Never Said a Mumblin' Word

Lenten
Meditations on
the Spirituals

Mark Francisco Bozzuti-Jones

Augsburg Fortress
Minneapolis

Dedicated to

Muriel Jestina Townsend,
my mother who sang me
all these spirituals and more

And my wife,
Kathy

All Scripture quotations are from New Revised Standard Version Bible, copyright © 1989 Division of Christian Education of the National Council of the Churches of Christ in the United States of America. Used by permission.

Excerpt from "Redemption Song," by Bob Marley, copyright © 1980 Fifty-Six Hope Road Music Ltd./Odnil Music Ltd./Blue Mountain Music Ltd. (PRS). All rights controlled and administered by Rykomusic Inc (ASCAP). All rights reserved. Lyrics used by permission.

Editors: Ronald S. Bonner, Scott Tunseth, James Satter

Cover art: *The Mourners*, by Fred Flemister, courtesy the Clark Atlanta University Art Gallery
Cover design: Shalette Cauley-Wandrick
Text design: Carolyn Berge

ISBN 0-8066-4555-5

The paper used in this publication meets the minimum requirements of American National Standard for Information Sciences—Permanence of Paper for Printed Library Materials, ANSI Z329.48-1984.

Manufactured in the U.S.A.

06   05   04   03   02   1   2   3   4   5   6   7   8   9   10

Prelude

Lent is not an easy time. It is a time for us to stretch ourselves. Stretching or lengthening our lives can involve a lot of pain and "death." But even more important than pain and death is faith. We need faith to believe that as we experience the ashes of life, life can and will rise from those ashes. Liberation awaits us. Freedom calls us throughout Lent.

Spirituals offer the opportunity for all of us to look at the ashes of our existence. We meditate on these words because we know that the slavery of some has been more painful than others. We meditate on these spirituals because we believe there is resurrection in opening ourselves to the suffering and pain in our lives and others'.

The experience of Yahweh as liberator holds tremendous importance for the Jewish people in light of their experience of suffering and oppression. In their darkest hour they find Yahweh on their side working for their liberation. They sing the praises of Yahweh even as they suffer. Their scriptures reflect their struggle to understand what it means to be the chosen people in light of their suffering.

Christians also give a tremendous attention to suffering. As Christians, we oftentimes describe Jesus as the suffering servant of Isaiah. We remember his resurrection, but we never try to deny the suffering of God.

Black people, throughout the world, have suffered all manner of evil. Throughout their suffering, they have found a voice to await and proclaim God's love and liberation. In these spirituals, I offer the reader a chance to find God in the words of slaves who never stopped believing in God's love.

Lent offers us a chance to rededicate ourselves to God. We are called to identify with Jesus as the Suffering Slave. As we meditate on Jesus, we are called to be change agents in this world. May these spirituals aid our journey as we struggle with what it means to be a people of God. May we find Jesus in them, and may we find ourselves, too. Take time to read the spirituals; they speak volumes of a God who is both ancient and new.

Wouldn't it be divine if we could sing and praise in the midst of suffering, even as we work out our liberation? These spirituals provide deep insight into the hearts, minds, and souls of a people, who like us, struggle to make sense of suffering and the promise of new life.

Spend time with these songs; they are much more than a mumbalin' word.

DAY **1** | ASH WEDNESDAY

He Never Said a Mumbalin' Word

They crucified my Lord,
And He never said a mumbalin' word;
They crucified my Lord,
And He never said a mumbalin' word.
Not a word, not a word, not a word.

They nailed him to a tree,
And He never said a mumbalin' word;
They nailed him to a tree,
And He never said a mumbalin' word.
Not a word, not a word, not a word.

They pierced Him in the side,
And He never said a mumbalin' word;
They pierced Him in the side,
And He never said a mumbalin' word.
Not a word, not a word, not a word.

He hung His head and died,
And He never said a mumbalin' word;
He hung His head and died,
And He never said a mumbalin' word.
Not a word, not a word, not a word.

Traditional

It is no accident that the ashes on Ash Wednesday are from last year's Passion Sunday. "Remember that you are dust and to dust you shall return." When the celebrant utters these words there is no response. It is a subtle reminder that before our frailty we stand in awe or silence. At times life hurts so hard that we become numb.

Ash Wednesday offers the only time throughout the year when we get dirty in church. We are marked with ashes. Can we find the words in our hearts that speak to a condition of ashes? To be touched with ashes is to remember the lives of so many people who have been hurt and discarded by society. We may choose to be silent as we are marked with the ashes. But should we be silent in the face of the suffering of others?

We are marked with the cross. Imagine the lives scarred by hate, rejection, suffering, slavery, and war. God calls us on Ash Wednesday to note the frailty of humanity. In our hearts, we should mark a cross this day. "He never said a mumbalin word" reminds us that at times, all of us are struck dumb by suffering. But we are called to help carry the cross of others and not just talk about it. Lent calls us to look closely at the cross that marks us.

Throughout his passion, Jesus remains relatively silent. His words, according to the Gospel writers, give deep insight into his love for God and those around him, even his persecutors. "He never said a mumbalin' word." Maybe we can imitate Jesus' silence.

In a world so dominated by noise and activities, how different our lives would be if we found time to be quiet. We have gotten so used to talking and have grown accustomed to listening to the words of others. When was the last time we took time to listen to our hearts?

Jesus said few words during his trial and as he approached his death. What was he thinking? What was he feeling? We may get an insight into Jesus' action if we join him in being quiet.

His mother, Mary, is also noticeably silent during this time. Scriptures portray her as "pondering" the mysteries of life in her heart.

May we come to discover the mystery of our life by being quiet.

Spiritual Exercise

See whether during these forty days you can open yourself up to five or ten minutes of quiet time each day. Find a quiet place and see whether you can still your mind and just be aware of God's presence in your life. Try to notice what happens when you still your heart and your lips.

- Have you said something lately that was not true or kind that caused someone pain? Reflect on the experience of that moment and ask for God's grace to make amends.

- What are the things you "mumble" to yourself? Can you share them with the Lord?

- Remember, God is interested in what you have to say.

DAY **2** | THURSDAY

I Want to Be Ready

I want to be ready, I want to be ready.
I want to be ready to walk in Jerusalem
Just like John.

John said that Jerusalem was four square,
Walk in Jerusalem just like John.
I hope, good Lord, I'll meet you there,
Walk in Jerusalem just like John.

When Peter was preaching at Pentecost,
Walk in Jerusalem just like John.
O he was filled with the Holy Ghost,
Walk in Jerusalem just like John.

Traditional

W hat does it mean for us to be ready? What does it take for us to get ready? The Gospel of John refers to one of the disciples as the one whom Jesus loved. In this spiritual, there is reference to walking just like John.

Maybe, being ready implies accepting that we are loved by God. It is true; we are loved unconditionally by God. It is this love that should inspire us to get ready to "talk the talk and walk the walk."

The line "walk in Jerusalem just like John" invites us to seek peace and love in our daily lives. John walks in the city of peace because he followed Jesus and rested on the bosom of Jesus.

As a way of getting ready, we may spend some time examining the things that prevent us from loving ourselves, our family, our neighbors, and God.

Spiritual Exercise

Spend a few minutes today examining your head. I mean that. John rested his head on Jesus' bosom. Make a list of five things that remind you of God's love. Spend a few minutes thanking God for these gifts, graces, or people. Also, take some time to look at three things that deprive you of peace, hope, or confidence.

Spend time thanking God for the things on your lists. Yes, thank God.

- Where do you rest your head?
- What's in your head?
- Remember that God wants to be a part of what is in your head.

DAY **3** | FRIDAY

I Love the Lord

I love the Lord, He heard my cry and pitied every groan.
Long as I live and troubles rise,
I'll hasten to his throne.

I love the Lord, He heard my cry and pitied every groan.
O let my heart no more despair
While I have breath to pray.

Traditional

When was the last time we declared our love for God? "I Love the Lord" is a spiritual that did not originate in a time of peace and tranquility, but instead grew out of tremendous suffering and pain.

The liberation theologians of Latin America share the experience of working with the extreme poor who never lose their belief in God. It is easy to love our jobs, our families, and even ourselves when things are going well. What does it mean to love when faced with sickness, pain, defeat, and the mysteries of life?

Each Lent, we have the opportunity to reflect on the mystery of suffering and pain. It is very important that we notice our own pain and suffering, and just as important that we notice how we contribute to pain and suffering in the lives of others.

Spiritual Exercise

Spend some time today asking the Lord for the grace and the courage to be faithful in the midst of pain, suffering, and temptations. Saint Ignatius of Loyola encouraged the Jesuits to imagine the poor and suffering throughout the world.

Notice what happens in your heart when you think of the pain and suffering of others.

Take a few moments to imagine that God is seeing the world through your eyes. See whether you can notice how God feels about pain and suffering. You might want to give yourself a longer time to do this exercise.

■ Is there suffering and pain in your family?

■ How might God be calling you to address the pain in your family?

■ Remember that God is with you.

DAY **4** | SATURDAY

Somebody's Knockin' at Your Door

Somebody's knockin' at your door;
Somebody's knockin' at your door.
O sinner, why don't you answer?
Somebody's knockin' at your door.

Knocks like Jesus, somebody's knockin' at your door;
Knocks like Jesus, somebody's knockin' at your door.
O sinner, why don't you answer?
Somebody's knockin' at your door.

Can't you hear him? Somebody's knockin' at your door;
Can't you hear him? Somebody's knockin' at your door.
O sinner, why don't you answer?
Somebody's knockin' at your door.

Jesus calls you, somebody's knockin' at your door;
Jesus calls you, somebody's knockin' at your door.
O sinner, why don't you answer?
Somebody's knockin' at your door.

Can't you trust Him? Somebody's knockin' at your door;
Can't you trust Him? Somebody's knockin' at your door.
O sinner, why don't you answer?
Somebody's knockin' at your door.

Traditional

Every now and again our doorbell rings unexpectedly. In these moments, I love to watch my wife. She becomes quiet, and I can see her wondering who is on the other side. Should she open the door? Oftentimes, she turns and looks at me and I raise my shoulders. Sometimes we sit quietly until the person goes away. If a friend does not call in a few days to say, "I came by to visit," we decide it was an uninvited salesperson.

In this spiritual, Jesus is knockin' and calling out to us. In Jamaica, when somebody calls out your name the correct response is, "What are you calling me for?" Something in the human spirit wants to know why a person is knockin' at the door.

"Can't you trust him?" It is hard to trust, because life and people are oftentimes unpredictable. Maybe that's why we don't always open the door to strangers who knock. We fear the unknown. Things do not happen the way we want them to happen and when we want them to happen. It must not be easy for Jesus to keep knockin', especially when so many people refuse to open their doors to him. How can we help others recognize his voice?

Spiritual Exercise

Spend a few moments today reflecting on what calls out to you. List five things that constantly demand your attention. Put them in a bowl and offer them to Jesus.

Jesus said, "I have come that you might have life." It may be worthwhile to find out what kind of life Jesus is talking about.

- Why don't we answer the door?
- What makes us neglect opportunities for growth, love, and change?
- Remember, if you open the door, Jesus will come in.

Great Day

Great day! Great day, the righteous marching.
Great day.

Chariot rode on the mountain top,
My God spoke and the chariot did stop,
God's going to build up Zion's walls!

This is the day of jubilee,
The Lord has set his people free,
God's going to build up Zion's walls!

We want no cowards in our band,
We call for valiant hearted men,
God's going to build up Zion's walls!

Going to take a breast plate, sword and shield
And march out boldly in the field,
God's going to build up Zion's walls!

Traditional

The Sundays in Lent are not traditionally counted as part of the forty-day Lenten journey. Even during Lent, Sundays are a time of celebration when we join other members of our Christian community in giving thanks to God. In worship, we hear of the temptation of Jesus (Matthew 4:1-11; Luke 4:1-13) or of his baptism (Mark 1:9-15). It would be good to spend time today with one of these passages. It is a great day. Jesus does not give in to the temptations. Great day. Jesus is baptized and called God's son. We share this baptism, and God calls us "child." Great day.

There is a lot of drama in the descriptions of Jesus facing the forces of evil. In the desert, Jesus is tempted to abandon the plan of God. We learn a lot about what it means to be tempted and to remain faithful. Jesus refuses to give in to immediate desires and pleasures, and instead he chooses to "worship" God in his decisions. It is a great day, because Jesus refuses to make hasty decisions to satisfy present-day needs. Jesus seems capable of seeing how his actions will affect his future mission.

When we focus on Jesus, we might learn to make decisions not to satisfy present-day needs, but to choose actions that lead to freedom, a greater life, and the glory of God. From where do we draw strength to act in this way? From the waters of baptism, where we are united with both the death and resurrection of Jesus (Romans 6:3-4).

Spiritual Exercise

It is great when we face our demons, weaknesses, pain, and failings—the things that enslave us. To look at where we are trapped provides insight into where freedom lies. Looking at our weakness and temptations can frighten us, but if we invite Jesus to journey with us we can experience hope.

Our church communities can also help us in our journey. We are not alone; we are all redeemed sinners.

Spend a few moments examining your most persistent temptations. For example, look at how pride, power, and money influence your life. Invite the Holy Spirit to lead you and remind you of God's love for you.

- What gives you a feeling of greatness in your life as a Christian?
- How do you help others in their moments of weakness?
- Remember that Jesus began his ministry after facing his demons.

DAY **5** | MONDAY

I Want Jesus to Walk with Me

I want Jesus to walk with me;
I want Jesus to walk with me;
All along my pilgrim journey,
Lord, I want Jesus to walk with me.

In my trials, Lord, walk with me;
In my trials, Lord, walk with me;
When the shades of life are falling,
Lord, I want Jesus to walk with me.

In my sorrows, Lord, walk with me;
In my sorrows, Lord, walk with me;
When my heart within is aching,
Lord, I want Jesus to walk with me.

Traditional

Sometimes we forget that our lives should be open to the word of God. God speaks to us daily, if we stop to listen. We also believe that God listens to us. God listens to our desires, dreams, and hopes. An ancient collect says it best: "Lord, to you all hearts are open, all desires known."

Today's spiritual expresses the profound and gentle desire to have Jesus be a companion on the journey. "Lord, walk with me" should become our mantra as a believing people.

"When my heart is aching, Lord, I want Jesus to walk with me"—this is a great invitation to examine how, where, and why our hearts ache, and to invite Jesus to walk with us.

Openness to the word of God gives us awareness around suffering and pain. Every child is born out of pain. New birth and new life spring from pain. So the place of the Christian is at the cross, helping to bring liberation. God desires to walk with us, because God knows that humans are made of dust, even though we breathe the breath of God.

Ironically, many of us are tempted to ignore God during the moments when things are going well. In Jamaica, the older people respond to any greeting with, "Give thanks!" It is important to thank God for the good times and the bad, and to ask for courage to walk with God whatever may come our way.

Spiritual Exercise

Repeat the lines of this spiritual throughout the day; then find a particular situation in your life and invite Jesus to walk with you. For example, "In my concerns about providing for my family, I want Jesus to walk with me."

Opening up our hearts in faith to God brings tremendous awareness, clarity, and peace. This is a great habit to develop: inviting Jesus to walk with you during the moments of temptations and trial. Ignatius of Loyola encouraged his Jesuit brothers to imagine that they were on their deathbed with ten minutes to live. He then invited them to imagine the beginning of their lives and to see Jesus walking with them in every single event of their lives.

- "When my heart within is aching"—What aching do you feel in your heart?

- When was the last time you shared with someone your journey with God?

- Remember that God is the one who walks with us.

DAY **6** | TUESDAY

Never Get Weary Yet

I never get weary yet;
I never get weary yet.
I've been down in the valley
A very long time,
But I never get weary yet.

We never get weary yet;
We never get weary yet.
We've been down in the valley
A very long time,
But we never get weary yet.

I am trodding on to Mt. Zion;
I am trodding on to Mt. Zion.
We've been down in the valley
A very long time,
But I never get weary yet.

We don't care what Babylon say;
We don't care what Babylon say.
We've been down in the valley
A very long time,
But we never get weary yet.

Jamaican Traditional

So much of life consists of making promises and vows to accomplish certain ends. We commit to diets, to exercise, to change bad habits, to start new projects, and to take vacation time. As humans, we often find that persevering is easier said than done. Midway through our commitments we give way to sleep, distractions, or to some other project.

This spiritual reminds us of the importance of not giving up. No matter how rocky the road gets, it is important that we keep going.

I met an older woman once who said the same prayer every Sunday. I attended eucharist at her nursing home for five years, and every day the woman would say the same prayer. Her prayer was this: "Lawd, may we never grow weary of well doing!" People grew resentful of her saying the same thing every day, so they asked me to talk to her. Of course, I did not. Today, after many years, it is this prayer that I remember.

Spiritual Exercise

Spend some time walking around your home or your office and look at all the things you have done. Give thanks to God for all your accomplishments, even those that had a short life span.

In the rite of confession, there is a line that says, "Things done and left undone." Take a few moments to reread this spiritual, and then think of all the things you have done that give you energy or drain your energy.

Maybe this is a good time for you to commit to doing something creative, kind, or healthy.

If possible, skip a meal today or tomorrow and notice what happens.

- What makes you stay down in the valley?
- Reflect on what it means to never get weary of well-doing.
- Remember that the Lord is your strength and salvation.

DAY **7** | WEDNESDAY

Ezek'el Saw de Wheel

Ezek'el saw de wheel
'Way up in de middle o' de air,
Ezek'el saw de wheel
'Way in de middle o' de air.
De big wheel run by faith,
De little wheel by de grace o' God;
A wheel in a wheel
'Way in de middle o' de air.

Better min', my sister, how you walk on de cross,
Way in de middle o' de air,
Yo' foot might slip an' yo' soul be los'
'Way in de middle o' de air.

Let me tell you, brother, what a sinner will do,
'Way in de middle o' de air,
He'll step on me an' he'll step on you
'Way in de middle o' de air.

Traditional

We often forget the importance of faith and grace in our lives. At times we want lofty and technical explanations for grace and faith, and then forget that they are alive in every waking moment. We need to remind ourselves to be open to the work of God.

Ezekiel is remembered as the prophet who told that the Israelites would reap devastation because of their unwillingness to be open to God during their captivity. But he also envisioned many great and wonderful things for the people of God, because of God's unchanging love for them.

This spiritual offers a vision of grace and faith as being "way in de middle o' de air." It challenges us to think about where we find grace and faith. The singers of this song must have looked up to the heavens as they sang. As God's people, we are called to know the places and people who remind us why we have faith and grace.

There is a lot of warning in this song. We often do not like to be warned about danger, but danger exists in this world. And so do consequences for our actions. Sometimes we can increase our faith and be more aware of grace in our daily lives, if we listen to the advice of the wise people around.

Spiritual Exercise

Imagine a time in your life when you experienced a profound sense of God's grace or your faith in God. Recall that day or that moment. See whether you can recall your feelings, the people, the words, and the joy of that moment.

Stay in the moment of that memory and recall how that moment deepened your faith in God and made you more aware of God's grace. What lessons from this experience still influence your life today?

Read Ezekiel 1:1-28.

- How do you influence the faith of others?

- Where do you see faith and grace in your life and in your family?

- Remember that grace increases in moments of trial, temptation, and failure.

DAY **8** | **THURSDAY**

Bye and Bye

O bye and bye, bye and bye,
I'm gonna lay down my heavy load.

I know my robe's gonna fit me well,
I'm gonna lay down my heavy load.
I tied it on at the gates of hell.
I'm gonna lay down my heavy load.

O hell is deep and in dark despair,
I'm gonna lay down my heavy load.
So stop, po' sinner and don't go there.
I'm gonna lay down my heavy load.

O Christian, can't you arise and tell,
I'm gonna lay down my heavy load.
That Jesus hath done all things well.
I'm gonna lay down my heavy load.

Traditional

"Come away with me and rest a while." "Come to me all who have heavy burdens." Jesus said these words quite frequently to his disciples. These words show a Jesus who is attuned to the burdens that accompany the human heart.

Jesus must have recognized that the disciples needed a break from it all, that they needed to rest and reflect. So many things burden our hearts, even religious thoughts can be too heavy at times. In this spiritual, we are invited to lay our burdens at the feet of God, who is always there to receive them. Ironically, it seems we cling most tightly to the things we need to let go.

Jesus also invites us to spend quiet time with him and rest in his presence. One summer I spent time visiting several churches that were nearly empty on Sundays. When I finally asked why, I was told that it was vacation time. One rector told me that even God had gone on vacation.

Sabbath rest does not mean ignoring the Sabbath, of course! But sabbath rest is something we need each day. We need to quiet our minds and lives enough to listen for God, to become more aware of God's presence and action, even on our vacation.

Spiritual Exercise

Make a list of three or four things that have troubled you lately. Next to each item, write and complete the following: "Jesus, I want you to. . . ."

At another time during the day, try to sit still for a few minutes. Recall the three or four items you listed and what you asked Jesus to do about them. Spend a few moments thanking God for listening to your prayer. Then spend a few more moments imagining what your life would be like if these three or four things did not exist in your life.

Close this day's meditation with a portion of the Serenity Prayer attributed to Reinhold Neibuhr:

> God grant me the serenity
> to accept the things I cannot change,
> courage to change the things I can,
> and wisdom to know the difference.

- What are your most prized possessions? Do you know why?
- What things in your life require more determination to lay down?
- Remember that God does all things well and works in mysterious ways.

Key Man

A pair of every animal
Was saved in the ark,
Saved in the ark,
Saved in the ark.

A pair of every animal
Was saved in the ark.

Key man, lock the door an' gone;
Key man, key man, key man, key man.
Key man, lock the door an' gone;
Key man, key man, key man, key man.
Key man, lock the door an' gone.

Jamaican Traditional

Noah remains one of the most puzzling biblical figures. God chose him to preserve life by collecting all living things before the flood. It is almost impossible to put our minds around this story. What really happened? Did the flood destroy the whole earth? How did all the animals get along in the ark? How did the humans survive the stench?

The million-dollar question is *why*?

In this Jamaican spiritual, the name Noah is never mentioned. Instead, he is called the "key man." Jamaicans like the story of the flood, but they cannot understand Noah's lack of compassion. He locked the door and left. As a child, I kept asking the teacher, "What happened to the people outside?" The teacher replied, "That is not a part of the story."

Noah and the flood give us a lot of food for thought during this season of Lent. It is always a good thing to ask about the people outside. We sometimes become so focused on our needs that we forget the needs of others. It is always good to remember that there are people outside the church, outside our nation, and outside our ethnic group.

Spiritual Exercise

Read the story of Noah in Genesis 6:1—9:29.

Take a few moments to quiet your mind. Imagine that you watched Noah building the ark. Notice your feelings toward Noah and his family.

Now imagine that you and your family were left out of the ark. See Noah closing the door and going in. What does this feel like to be left out of the ark? Since the story tells us that those left out of the ark died, think about the people in poor communities and in poor nations who are left out of the ark of health care, job benefits, and decisions.

■ How do we decide whom to include and invite into our church? Our homes? Our lives?

■ Why is it easy to dismiss others?

■ Remember that Jesus cares for all people.

DAY **10** | SATURDAY

Better Be Ready

Better be ready; better be ready; better be ready;
Ready to try on your long white robe.

Oh rise up children, get your crown,
And by your Savior's side sit down.

What a glorious morning that will be,
Our friends and Jesus, we shall see.

O shout you Christians, you're gaining ground,
We'll shout old Satan's kingdom down!

I soon shall reach that golden shore,
And sing the songs we sang before.

Traditional

L ent is a time to recommit to God and to rediscover ourselves in God. It is a time to take an honest look at our lives and an honest look at God in our lives. These forty days are a time to make our hearts ready for the Lord. John the Baptist emphasized the importance of making a straight path for God. How we get ready to meet and experience God is an important part of Lent.

In the play *Hamlet* Shakespeare wrote, "the readiness is all." If we prepare ourselves for life, then the surprise we encounter might take on a different quality. We get ready for business meetings, we get ready for dinners and parties, we get ready for guests, but few of us get ready for God. For whatever reason, we as a Christian people have lost the sense of what it means to get ready for worship. In addition, we give little importance to spiritual, theological, or biblical readiness.

The words of this spiritual invite us to think about getting ready and what it means to be ready. Lent is a preparation for Easter, but it is also a preparation for us to experience an Easter of our own. "What a glorious morning that will be, our friends and Jesus we will see." We can hope that by the time Easter comes (or any experience of God) we will have a more profound sense of God's glory in our lives.

Spiritual Exercise

"Oh rise up children, get your crown / And by your Savior's side sit down." Lent is a time to sit by Jesus' side.

Take some time today to sit next to Jesus. Imagine that you are in a quiet place, such as a garden or on the beach. From a short distant you can see Jesus sitting alone. He notices your presence and invites you to come over. See yourself walking over to Jesus. Notice what Jesus is wearing and notice the sound of his voice as he calls your name. As you sit next to Jesus, listen to what he has to say to you.

■ What does it mean to get ready for God, for church, and for the spiritual life?

■ How is this Lent different from the previous years?

■ Remember that God is ready for you.

Oh, Freedom!

Oh, freedom! Oh, freedom, Oh freedom
Over me!
An befo' I'd be a slave
I'll be buried in my grave,
An' go home to my Lord an' be free.

No mo' moanin', No mo' moanin', No mo' moanin'
Over me!
An befo' I'd be a slave
I'll be buried in my grave,
An' go home to my Lord an' be free.

No mo' weepin', No mo' weepin', No mo' weepin'
Over me!
An befo' I'd be a slave
I'll be buried in my grave,
An' go home to my Lord an' be free.

There'll be prayin', There'll be prayin', There'll be prayin'
Over me!
An' befo' I'd be a slave
I'll be buried in my grave,
An' go home to my Lord and be free.

Traditional

This spiritual has tremendous implications for us as we journey through Lent. Over and over, the line "befo' I'd be a slave, I'll be buried in my grave" appears. It haunts us because it reminds us of the tragic stain on our human history. We cannot and should not deny the horrible acts that happened during slavery and the tremendous impact they have on all of us today.

But what is most interesting about this song is the repetition of "befo' I'd be a slave." The song's original singers lived as slaves. So what could this song mean? Dr. Horace Boyer explains that this song is more about slavery to sin. The slaves who believed in Jesus thought slavery to sin was worse than the physical slavery in which they lived.

Could the slaves have been singing to their masters, reminding them that their slavery would come in the next life? For these slaves freedom was found in Jesus and in their ability to sing to God. We are reminded of the people of Israel in Egypt.

As we continue with our journey through Lent, we might benefit by examining what enslaves us in this life and what offers us freedom. In his "Redemption Song," the legendary Jamaican singer Bob Marley sings, "Emancipate yourselves from mental slavery, none but ourselves can free our minds. Have no fear for atomic energy, for none of them can stop the times."

We sometimes forget that the effects of mental slavery can be just as powerful as physical slavery.

Spiritual Exercise

Make a list of qualities that would describe a person who is free from most mental, spiritual, and emotional baggage.

Take some time to quiet yourself. In your mind, go back to some unpleasant event in your past. Approach this exercise with self-knowledge, knowing your pain threshold for past experiences.

As you reflect on this experience, place yourself next to Jesus as he prays in the garden before his trial. See the agony he is experiencing. Imitate Jesus. Kneel next to him. If he prays out loud, pray aloud, too. When he is quiet, remain quiet. Do not speak to him. Just imitate his moment of suffering.

■ What enslaves your spirit and your mind? How can you be free?

■ What are you afraid to admit about why you remain enchained spiritually, mentally, and physically?

■ Remember that in Jesus there is true freedom; he calls you to be free.

DAY **11** | MONDAY

Wayfaring Stranger

I'm just a poor wayfaring stranger,
I'm trav'ling through this world below;
There is no sickness, toil, nor danger,
In that bright world to which I go.
I'm going there to see my father,
I'm going there no more to roam;
I'm just a going over Jordan,
I'm just a going over home.

I know dark clouds will gather o'er me,
I know my pathway's rough and steep;
But golden fields lie out before me,
Where weary eyes no more shall weep.
I'm going there to see my mother,
She said she'd meet me when I come;
I'm just a going over Jordan,
I'm just a going over home.

I want to sing salvation's story,
In concert with the blood-washed band;
I want to wear a crown of glory,
When I get home to that good land.
I'm going there to see my brothers,
They passed before me one by one;
I'm just a going over Jordan,
I'm just a going over home.

I'll soon be free from every trial,
This form will rest beneath the sod;
I'll drop the cross of self-denial,
And enter in my home with God.
I'm going there to see my Savior,
Who shed for me His precious blood;
I'm just a going over Jordan,
I'm just a going over home.

Traditional

Critics of Christianity argue that it falsely offers hope for the future. They claim that Christianity advocates a better life in the future, while inadequately addressing the misery of the present life.

Many missionaries in the past preached Christianity (at least some aspects) as a means of maintaining the status quo. What is undeniable is that Christianity provided a glimpse of a better life in the future, but also hope for a better life on earth. The experience of the Israelites, once the slaves grew familiar with the story, taught them that God was interested in their liberation.

The civil rights movement in the United States and the liberation theologies of Latin America are present-day examples of Christianity encouraging the struggle for a better life in the here and now.

From "Wayfaring Stranger" we realize that sometimes the more things change the more they remain the same. In today's society, with all its technological advances, we are still in need of dreaming of a better tomorrow. Christianity reminds us that death is not the final word. From that message we can learn that God's dream for us is that we have life, in the here and now, in all its abundance.

"I'm just a going over Jordan, I'm just a going over home" calls to mind the baptism of Jesus in the Jordan River and of our own baptism, which makes us full members of the body of Christ. As "wayfaring strangers," we live to serve in this life now, even as we look ahead to that other everlasting home Jesus has prepared for us.

Spiritual Exercise

Reflect on your baptism. When did it happen? Who was present? Were you an infant, child, teenager, young adult, or adult? How does your baptism inform your faith and your life?

Look into your heart and consider what it means to be a "wayfaring stranger." If this life is but a temporary home, how can you make it the best home possible?

Ask Jesus to be with you in your "pilgrim" journey.

- What signs reveal to you that God walks with you in your life?
- What has your experience as a "wayfaring stranger" been?
- Remember that Jesus was poor, homeless, the son of a pregnant teenager, abandoned by his friends, and viewed as a failure by many.

DAY **12** | TUESDAY

It's Me

It's me, it's me, O Lord,
Standin' in the need of prayer;
It's me, it's me, O Lord.
Standin' in the need of prayer.

Not my brother, not my sister, but it's me, O Lord,
Standin' in the need of prayer.
Not my brother, not my sister, but it's me, O Lord,
Standin' in the need of prayer.

Not the preacher, not the deacon, but it's me, O Lord,
Standin' in the need of prayer.
Not the preacher, nor the deacon, but it's me, O Lord,
Standin' in the need of prayer.

Not my father, not my mother, but it's me, O Lord,
Standin' in the need of prayer.
Not my father, not my mother, but it's me, O Lord,
Standin' in the need of prayer.

Not the stranger, not my neighbor, but it's me, O Lord,
Standin' in the need of prayer.
Not the stranger, not my neighbor, but it's me, O Lord,
Standin' in the need of prayer.

Traditional

hen Barbara Clementine Harris was first nominated to be Suffragan Bishop in the Episcopal Diocese of Massachusetts, she never believed that she would be elected, approved, and ordained a bishop. She said publicly that when the Church spoke about ordaining women, they were talking about white women as bishops.

Even before the convention to elect the bishop, many called up Barbara and simply said, "We are praying for you. You will succeed." Barbara still did not believe, but she began to enjoy the feeling that tens of thousands of people around the world were praying for her. After her ordination as bishop, she thanked all the people who brought her before God in prayer.

We sometimes forget the power of prayer. I feel fortunate to be able to say my family prays for me every day. At five o'clock every morning, my mother is praying for me. And I need it. We need the prayers of others, and others need our prayers. We must never grow tired of owning our need for prayer, asking others to pray for specific things in our life, and praying for others.

In this spiritual, we get a reminder of our need for prayer. The singer reminds God that it is not the others who are in need of prayer, but the singer herself. It is almost as though the singer wants God to pray for her. And is this not what we believe that Jesus does? Imagine that Jesus prays for us all the time.

Spiritual Exercise

Make a list of people whom you would like to pray for, and then make a list of people you have a difficult time liking. Spend some time praying for both groups of people. Pay attention to what happens when you pray in this way.

Ask the Lord to reveal to you something you need to do for or say to one or more of the people on these lists. Pray for the grace to do it. It might simply be calling up the person and saying, "I love you," "Thank you," or "I'm sorry."

- Do you stand in the need of prayer? What are your needs?

- What do you want to be happy? What do you need to be happy?

- Remember that you are in the heart of God and that Jesus prays for you with every breath you take.

DAY **13** | WEDNESDAY

Down by the Riverside

I'm gonna lay down my burden, down by the riverside,
Down by the riverside, down by the riverside.
I'm gonna lay down my burden, down by the riverside,
And I ain't gonna study war no more.
I ain't gonna study war no more.

I'm gonna lay down my sword and shield, down by the riverside,
Down by the riverside, down by the riverside.
I'm gonna lay down my sword and shield, down by the riverside,
And I ain't gonna study war no more.
I ain't gonna study war no more.

I'm gonna put on my long white robe, down by the riverside,
Down by the riverside, down by the riverside.
I'm gonna to put on my long white robe, down by the riverside,
And I ain't gonna study war no more.
I ain't gonna study war no more.

Traditional

We all have burdens to bear. One of my mother's favorite sayings was, "God never gives us more than we can bear." That was her strongest belief. In it she affirmed that we all have a burden or a cross, but that God always gives us the grace to bear it. In my mother's worldview, God knew everything, especially how much each person could bear. How would we respond to my mother's statement today? Do some people receive more than they can bear?

There is a story about two monks on a journey. They came upon a river that was difficult to cross. A woman, known to be a prostitute, was there and she asked to be taken across. Without hesitation, one of the monks had her climb on his back, and so the three of them crossed the river together. On the other side, the woman went on her way. The monks walked in silence for three hours. Finally one monk said, "I cannot believe you carried that woman across the river." The other replied, "My friend, I left the woman at the river, but I see she is still on your mind."

There are times when we need to "lay down" the burden of worry, manipulation, and cynicism. Jesus pointed to the lily of the fields and the birds of the air to enforce his lesson about not worrying. They neither "toil nor spin, but your heavenly Father provides for them." We all know that lilies and birds work a lot. So Jesus is not telling us not to worry or prepare for life. Jesus seeks to address the worries that burden the human heart, mind, and soul.

Sometimes the best way to experience freedom is to admit our limitations, in such a way that we do not judge others. Sometimes we may need a lot more than prayer to be freed from our burdens. We may need to seek help, or commit to a decision to change our patterns of thinking or behaving. The best way to do something is to begin it. The best way to stop carrying a burden is to put it down.

Spiritual Exercise

Spend time today being aware of the things that burden your heart, mind, and soul. Ask yourself the following questions: What burdens my heart? What burdens my mind? What burdens my soul?

You might find that this is the first time you have thought of the heart, mind, and soul as burdened. Stay with these questions and notice what happens as you reflect on your mental, physical, and spiritual state?

Make an act of confession—privately, to a friend, or to a pastor or priest. In today's world the art of confession has almost been lost, but you may find tremendous grace and freedom by confessing your sin. Sin has a way of burdening our soul. Sometimes, what burdens your heart may not be sinful, but may simply mirror the ups and downs of life. It is important to have someone to talk to about the things of our heart.

- Is there a burden you are finding too difficult to bear these days? What is God asking of you?

- How is the laying down of burdens related to turning away from studying war? How do the burdens we carry contribute to a "warring" mood?

- Remember that Jesus wants to help you with your burdens.

DAY **14** | **THURSDAY**

Give Me Jesus

In the morning when I rise,
In the morning when I rise,
In the morning when I rise,
Give me Jesus.

Give me Jesus, give me Jesus,
You may have all this world,
Give me Jesus.

Dark midnight was my cry,
Dark midnight was my cry,
Dark midnight was my cry,
Give me Jesus.

O when I come to die,
O when I come to die,
O when I come to die,
Give me Jesus.

Traditional

"Give me Jesus" is best understood as choosing Jesus over all else. Would we really give up our world to have Jesus? We get so caught up in our projects that we forget to make room for Jesus. A common complaint of parents is that their children have too many school activities, which prevent them from going to church.

The Christian life offers us many opportunities to choose Jesus. We sometimes miss these Jesus-moments because we are busy holding onto our world. This song affirms that the desire for Jesus should infuse our entire day: "in the morning, dark midnight, and when I come to die."

Many of us define ourselves by our intellectual achievements, our possessions, or our ability to do certain things. One of the best ways to get to know ourselves is to find out what we cling to. We *are* our desires, our needs, and wants.

Ignatius of Loyola, founder of the Jesuits, encouraged his brothers not only to see the will of God, but to work for the greater honor and glory of God. Ignatius wanted his followers to always desire Jesus. When one of his students told him he had no desire to choose Jesus, Ignatius asked him to "pray that you may have this desire."

To desire Jesus is one way to receive Jesus. In receiving Jesus, we are opened to the scriptures, to moments of grace, to acts of kindness, and to becoming faithful members of a community of faith.

Spiritual Exercise

Find a comfortable place to sit. Quiet yourself and try to be aware of your breath, your bodily sensations, and even the clothes resting on your body. Imagine that as you breathe in and out, you are breathing in the breath of God and breathing into God. Envision your breath (exhale) as entering into God's presence and see your breath (intake) as issuing from God's presence.

Now gently move your hands and rest them on your lap, palms facing upward, as if open to God. Make your movements very slow, like the opening of a rose. When your hands are resting on your lap, see whether you can be aware of the air touching your hands. Now raise your head very slowly and look up to the heavens. Stay in this position for a few minutes. Slowly repeat to yourself several times, "Jesus, I want you in my life!"

Repeat this exercise a few times.

- What does it mean to receive Jesus?
- Why is Jesus important to you?
- Remember that Jesus desires to fill your heart.

DAY **15** | FRIDAY

Calvary

Calvary, Calvary, Calvary, Calvary, Calvary,
Calvary, surely He died on Calvary.

Every time I think about Jesus,
Every time I think about Jesus,
Every time I think about Jesus,
Surely He died on Calvary.

Don't you hear the hammering,
Don't you hear the hammering,
Don't you hear the hammering,
Surely he died on Calvary.

Don't you hear Him calling His Father?
Don't you hear Him calling His Father?
Don't you hear Him calling His Father?
Surely He died on Calvary.

Traditional

In the early life of the Church, Fridays were a time of penance and soul searching. Lent offers us a chance to reflect on our suffering, pain, and challenges, but more than that it gives us a chance to reflect on Jesus' suffering, pain, and challenges.

As Christians, we want to identify more and more with Jesus. We are followers of Jesus because we believe that in Jesus we find life, hope, and a way of life that is abundant in grace. Following Jesus requires daily attention, and we can always learn something new. This Lent, let us learn from Jesus.

Jesus' reaction to pain, loss, betrayal, and rejection provide us with ample instructions on how to live our lives as Christians. As Christians, we do not deny the suffering of God. Each Sunday, we gather as a people to remember Christ's death.

"Surely he died on Calvary" reminds us of Jesus' death, or assassination, carried out through torture and crucifixion. This spiritual calls us back to the central part of our faith: there is no thinking about Jesus without thinking about Calvary. To follow Jesus is to remember Calvary and to embrace our experiences of Calvary.

Jesus accepted death willingly. Sometimes our experience of Calvary may require that we fight against oppression and injustice. To embrace and remember Calvary involves a strong commitment to peace, justice, and mercy.

Spiritual Exercise

Imagine a situation where injustice or a dire need for help exists. You may think of a person who is alone or who needs someone to talk to about a problem. You may think about groups that face great difficulty.

Then think of people around you in your family, your church, or your community who may be experiencing a Calvary. Expand your circle of caring outward. Think of people in need beyond your local reach.

Is there any cause that might be worth committing to as a means of bringing life or hope?

This may be a good time to look at a film on the life of Martin Luther King Jr., Mother Teresa, Oscar Romero, Desmond Tutu, or others who shared in the suffering of others. If you cannot find a video or a book about the life of one of these, see whether you can make a list of qualities these people had.

- Why did Jesus have to die?
- How is your pain and suffering tied to Jesus?
- Remember that Jesus was put to death.

DAY **16** | SATURDAY

Deep River

Deep river, my home is over Jordan,
Deep river, Lord, I want to cross over to camp ground.
Oh don't you want to go to that gospel feast,
That promised land where all is peace?
Oh deep river, Lord, I want to cross over to camp ground.

Traditional

When we allow our desires for God to take deep roots in our hearts, nothing is ever the same again. Our understanding of belonging to God changes everything we do, say, and think. For the Israelites in Egypt and the slaves in the Americas, knowing that their home was somewhere else gave them a lot of determination to be free. Moses articulated the desire for freedom, but he was not alone. The whole people of Israel gradually came to understand that God wanted them to be free. When they realized this, they committed to following Moses.

Throughout the history of slavery, many blacks and whites envisioned a world different from the one that existed. They had a dream that all people should go to the gospel feast. Martin Luther King Jr. energized the nation and the world to collaborate in the dream that God has for all people.

The life of Martin Luther King Jr. could be summed up by the questions he asked the United States. He asked the nation about their belief in God, their belief in equality and in justice.

Like Jesus, Martin Luther King Jr. gave his life for his dreams and questions. But even in death, he asked the question, "Oh don't you want to go to that gospel feast / That promised land where all is peace?" King believed that God wanted black Americans "to cross over to camp ground," into "that promise land where all is peace." We can learn from this struggle for justice, and we can ask God to help us transform our world.

Spiritual Exercise

Try to recall a moment when you felt very restless or agitated. You may want to imagine a situation in the past when you did not feel at home. The situation could have been at a family gathering, another social event, first day in a new school or job, or visiting a new nation. Recall those feelings, spend some time reliving the experience.

Now think about a change that you might need to make in your life. What "campground"—what new place of peace—do you need to cross into? How can you cross over? Repeat the words of the spiritual: "Deep river, my home is over Jordan / Deep river, Lord, I want to cross over to campground." Then be silent for a time.

Next, invite Jesus to be a part of that situation and see what Jesus has to say. Do not force the situation, just experience Jesus being with you as you listen. Repeat the words often during your time of prayer: "Lord, I want to cross over to camp ground. Help me cross. Show me the way."

Make these your last words before going to bed tonight or the first words you say as you wake up.

■ What do you want to say to God about the moments when you feel uncomfortable or oppressed?

■ What are your financial, emotional, and spiritual dreams? What part does Jesus play in them?

■ Remember that Jesus is God's gift of peace and the source of life-giving water.

THE THIRD SUNDAY IN LENT

Is There Anybody Here Who Loves My Jesus?

Is there anybody here who loves my Jesus?
Anybody here who loves my Lord?
I want to know if you love my Jesus;
I want to know if you love my Lord.

This world's a wilderness of woe,
So let us all to glory go.

Religion is a blooming rose,
And none but them who feel it know.

When I was blind and could not see,
King Jesus brought the light to me.

When every star refuses to shine,
I know King Jesus will be mine.

Traditional

I want to know if you love my Jesus." There are so many Christians in the world, and yet the world is far from fully experiencing the reign of God. When we say we love Jesus, what does that mean? Christians have many different ways to describe "loving Jesus."

Some people say that loving Jesus means engaging in acts of love. In Latin America, many theologians got into serious trouble with the Church, because they insisted that people who loved Jesus should work for a better world in the here and now. As the Lord's Prayer says, "Your will be done on earth as it is in heaven" (Matthew 6:10).

Others seem to separate our love for Jesus from our love for our brothers and sisters. But love connected to Jesus is both a vertical and a horizontal love. We can't look up without reaching out. Many of us would get embarrassed if we were asked about our love for Jesus. We view love as a private affair. We tend not to discuss love in public and are, even less inclined to discuss our love for others.

Lent is a time for us to question our love for God and to question what loving God entails. Do we love Jesus? Do we want to know if others love Jesus?

Spiritual Exercise

Read Luke 13:1-9. Write a poem or a letter to Jesus that best sums up your reaction to this Gospel text.

Then say the Lord's Prayer slowly and think about these lines from the spiritual: "Religion is a blooming rose / And none but them who feel it knows."

- Does your family love Jesus? How is this love for Jesus expressed?
- What do you think it means to love Jesus? What can you do to show your love for Jesus?
- Remember that Jesus invites us to abide in the love of God.

DAY **17** | MONDAY

My Lord, What a Morning

My Lord, what a morning,
My Lord, what a morning,
O my Lord, what a morning,
When the stars begin to fall.

You'll hear the trumpet sound,
To wake the nations under ground,
Looking to my God's right hand,
When the stars begin to fall.

You'll hear the sinner mourn
To wake the nations underground,
Looking to my God's right hand,
When the stars begin to fall.

You'll hear the Christian shout,
To wake nations underground,
Looking to my God's right hand,
When the stars begin to fall.

Traditional

ork can tire us and leave us without a zest for life. Many of us long for the weekend so that we can get away from the hustle and bustle of life at the office. Sometimes we just want to change gears and be in a different place. Weekends are usually time for us to recover and reenergize. For most of us, Monday comes around too quickly. We suffer from the "Monday morning blues."

We echo the words of this spiritual, oftentimes without being aware of it. Our whole body says, "My Lord, what a morning!" Yet, this song goes beyond a mere rough day at work or in life. It points to the end of the world "when the stars begin to fall." What a morning that will be when God returns at the end of time.

During Lent, we reflect on Jesus' death and all the events leading up to it. We sometimes forget that each day brings us closer to our own death. Death is a part of life and in many ways, as Anne Sexton said, life is an awful rowing toward God.

For Christians, the spiritual life offers us consolation. We are called to look to God's right hand. We know that a reference to the right hand of God is a reference to Jesus. In Jesus, we have a perfect example of how to accept not just suffering, but death. And we know that a bright morning awaits.

Spiritual Exercise

Have you ever imagined what the end of the world might look like? Find a quiet spot and think about it. You might even find it useful to draw a picture of what that day might look like.

When Jesus was on the cross, he uttered the words, "It is finished." Imagine that you are on your deathbed and were given fifteen minutes to get ready. What would you do to get ready for death? Whom would you want around you? What would be your final words?

After you have done this exercise, spend some time reflecting on your work or your life in general. Spend some time thanking God for the things you like about your job or situation, and pray for the situations or people you find difficult.

- What does it mean to be at God's right hand?

- If you could sit next to God for a while, what would you say or ask?

- Remember that Jesus is the Alpha and the Omega, the beginning and the end.

DAY **18** | TUESDAY

Swing Low, Sweet Chariot

Swing low, sweet chariot,
Coming for to carry me home.
Swing low, sweet chariot,
Coming for to carry me home.

I looked over Jordan, and what did I see
Coming for to carry me home.
A band of angels coming after me,
Coming for to carry me home.

If you get there before I do,
Coming for to carry me home.
Tell all my friends I'm coming too,
Coming for to carry me home.

The brightest day that ever I saw
Coming for to carry me home.
When Jesus wash'd my sins away,
Coming for to carry me home.

Traditional

The theme of dying comes up all the time during Lent, and rightly so. There is tremendous importance for us as Christians not to fear death but to welcome it. In ancient Christianity, there was always a prayer for a happy death. Sometimes the prayer was couched in a desire for peace. Praying for a peaceful death came from a belief that the holy person would die in a peaceful manner.

Praying about our death might strike some people as morbid, but it is a healthy reminder for us. We also remember that this is the note on which we begin Lent. "Remember that you are dust and to dust you shall return." Imagine if we said this phrase every day of our lives.

It may be helpful for us to ponder the words of an acclamation often used during the eucharist: "Dying you destroyed all death, rising you restored all life. Lord Jesus, come in glory." A close reading of the Gospels reveals that Jesus said a lot about his death. There is a lesson in this for all of us. We worship the living God, who died for us.

One of the ways we can think of death is to view it as the passageway into a more intimate experience and encounter with God. "Swing low, sweet chariot, coming for to carry me home." The spiritual reminds us that the chariot comes for all of us. Sickness and death form part of our experience as family. When we live in the awareness of this reality, we might find life, peace, and consolation more easily.

Spiritual Exercise

Spend some time thinking about your experience with pain, sickness, or death. If you sat next to someone and watched them die, relive that moment. You may try to recall visiting or sitting with a sick friend or relative. Or you may want to recall the moment when you heard of the death of a family member, close friend, or a well-known person.

Find a quiet space and quiet your thoughts. Try to recapture the thoughts and feelings you had at that moment. What words were said? What was the silence like? Looking back on this experience, what does it reveal to you about yourself? Ask the Lord to reveal to you the important lesson you need to learn or remember from this experience.

Repeat the words from the spiritual several times, each time more slowly: "The brightest day that ever I saw / Coming for to carry me home / When Jesus wash'd my sins away / Coming for to carry me home."

- Where is the sting of death in your life today? Where is God in all this?

- How do you think about your death? What would you like people to say about you when you are "gone"?

- Remember that Christ died so all may have life.

DAY **19** | WEDNESDAY

Daniel Saw the Stone

Daniel saw the stone
Rolling down to Babylon;
Daniel saw the stone
Rolling down to Babylon.
It was a great stone
Rolling down to Babylon.
Daniel saw the stone.

Jamaican Traditional

"Daniel saw the stone / Rolling down to Babylon." As prophets and seers go, Daniel is one of the most noteworthy in the history of Israel. Daniel interpreted dreams, challenged the political structures, was thrown in the lion's den, and through it all, modeled a life of faithfulness and attention to God.

We give tremendous importance to our eyes, our ability to see physical things. Most of us would find the lack of sight quite debilitating. I am reminded of a story Ray Charles has told. At a young age, he and his mother discovered that he had an eye condition that would lead to blindness. He recalled that his mother did not panic, but started to teach him how to get along without being able to see. His mother taught him how to judge space, how to be independent without sight. She gave him the gift of inner sight, he recalled.

Inner sight. That's a good way to describe seeing with the eyes of faith. When we seek vision though our mind, heart, and soul, we are best able to remain attuned to the working of God. Daniel saw visions of the past and the future. He saw the destruction of the power of Babylon, the power that had crushed Jerusalem and carried many of its people away into exile. Daniel offers us hope even as we live through rough moments. The "stone rolling down to Babylon" is the stone removed from the tomb of Jesus.

Lent is a good time to focus on increasing our spiritual inner sight. When we use our inner eyes of faith and prayer, we draw closer to the saving actions of God that are greater than any political, psychological, or physical power. Prayer and spiritual sight can bring us peace when we face the lions of life. There is a stone waiting to roll against all the things that oppress us and hold us in captivity. Ask God for the gift of Daniel. Ask God for the gift to see the stone rolling.

Spiritual Exercise

Go for a walk and try to find a stone, rock, or even a pebble. Sit quietly outside or in a quiet room. Look at the stone and imagine what thing in your life you would like to be knocked down or out by a huge stone. Imagine the stone you have in your hand increasing to a size that is far greater than any problem you might have. Then see this huge stone rolling over your problems and wiping them out.

Daniel was known as an interpreter of dreams, whose power to interpret came from his close relationship to God. What dreams, both positive and negative, are a part of you? How do your dreams match God's purposes for you?

- What spiritual "visions" have you had?

- It is nearly impossible to say the words "I have a dream" without thinking of Martin Luther King Jr.'s famous speech. What are your dreams?

- Remember these words of Jesus: "Blessed are those who have not seen and yet believe."

DAY **20** | **THURSDAY**

This Little Light of Mine

This little of mine,
I'm gonna let it shine,
This little of mine,
I'm gonna let it shine;
This little of mine,
I'm gonna let it shine,
Let it shine, let it shine, let it shine.

Every where I go,
I'm gonna let it shine,
Every where I go,
I'm gonna let it shine;
Every where I go,
I'm gonna let it shine,
Let it shine, let it shine, let it shine.

Jesus gave it to me,
I'm gonna let it shine,
Jesus gave it to me,
I'm gonna let it shine;
Jesus gave it to me,
I'm gonna let it shine,
Let it shine, let it shine, let it shine.

Traditional

Jesus told his followers that they should let their light so shine, that others would see their good works and give glory to God. In this spiritual there is a commitment to letting the light shine. Imagine shining a light for God in the midst of slavery?

When the Israelites found themselves enslaved and under dominion, there was always a prophet calling them to remain faithful. There is no denying that in the darkest hour, what we need most is a light. We speak about the light at the end of the tunnel, but at times we are too focused on the end of the tunnel. There is always need for us to shine a light now. "This little light of mine. I'm gonna let it shine!"

Don't worry that the light is "little." We sometimes want a big light, or we like to wait until we have a lot of power to put on a great show of light. There is merit in shining a little light. My mother used to say, "If you tarry until you are better, you will never come at all." I suspect she would say to all of us that if we wait until our light is big, we may never shine at all.

We all have moments of darkness, places in our lives that need light. It is consoling to know that we can shine our little light. Let the little light shine; it's all right. Many little lights combined will brighten the darkest of places.

Spiritual Exercise

Find a comfortable place to sit. Rest the palm of your hands on your legs facing upward to the heavens. Close your eyes and imagine that you are in a dark room. Feel the absence of light.

Now name something in your life that is draining light and life from you. Envision the darkness as the thing you name. For instance, you may name "Fear of groups," "Addiction to . . . ," "Anxieties," or whatever you choose. Imagine that as you sit or stand in that room, Jesus comes to you and gives you a small light. You might want to imagine Jesus saying, "My friend, I give you this small light. It won't go out, but it won't get bigger."

Notice what the little light does to the dark room. See what this light does to your fears, concerns, or pain.

Now name your light. Against fear, name your light courage. Against addiction, name your light freedom. Against overwork, name your light rest.

- Where does the light exist in your life?
- Who are the people who light up your life?
- Remember that Jesus brings light to the difficult places in your life.

DAY **21** | FRIDAY

Steal Away

Steal away, steal away, steal away to Jesus!
Steal away, steal away home, I ain't got long to stay here!

My Lord calls me,
He calls me by the thunder;
The trumpet sounds with-in-a my soul,
I ain't got long to stay here.

Green trees are bending,
Poor sinner stands a trembling;
The trumpet sounds with-in-a my soul,
I ain't got long to stay here.

Tomb stones are bursting,
Poor sinner stands a trembling;
The trumpet sounds with-in-a my soul,
I ain't got long to stay here.

My Lord calls me,
He calls me by the lighting;
The trumpet sounds with-in-a my soul,
I ain't got long to stay here.

Traditional

Once in a meeting of base community members in Brazil, I asked a child about God. Without missing a beat, the child said, "God is the liberator." For this group of Christians in Brazil, God wanted them to be free from the conditions that bring death. God was on their side in their fight for freedom from situations that oppressed them or caused death.

The government wanted to take their land away, and for this reason refused to supply them with water, electricity, and good roads. In addition, the government refused to set up a clinic in their neighborhood.

They gathered in church that evening. Asking themselves four questions: What is the situation before us? What do we think of it? What is God calling us to do? What is God going to do about it?

When we try to find out God's reaction to a situation and how we are called to respond as Christians, things take on a different perspective.

In this spiritual, the invitation is to steal away. The language is couched in the experience of death, but I suspect there is also a call to escape from slavery. "Give me liberty or give me death." It is probably hard for us to imagine a situation where death would be a welcome relief. Believe it or not, a majority of people in the world live in situations that cause them to die long before their time.

Lent is a good time to think about the millions of people who would love to steal away, but have nowhere to go.

Spiritual Exercise

Lie down on your bed or sit in your favorite chair. Experience how comfortable it is. Imagine what it must have been like to be an Israelite in Egypt, a slave in America, a prisoner in a concentration camp, or an indigenous person fighting for land.

In this exercise, try to create a movie or play about one of these situations, make yourself one of the lead actors, and see how things unfold.

When you have finished this exercise, thank God for the gift of freedom and all your blessings. You might make a decision to commit to a project that helps in the struggle for justice.

Repeat this exercise later in the day or some other time during Lent, but first begin with these lines: "Green trees are bending / Poor sinner stands a trembling / The trumpet sounds with-in-a my soul /I ain't got long to stay here."

- Why do people (or you) oppress others?
- If you could steal away, where would you go?
- Remember that God has heard and still hears the cries of the people.

DAY **22** | **SATURDAY**

Go Down, Moses

Go down, Moses, way down in Egypt's land;
Tell old Pharaoh to let my people go.

When Israel was in Egypt's land,
Let my people go;
Oppressed so hard, they could not stand,
Let my people go.

The Lord told Moses what to do,
Let my people go;
To lead the children of Israel through,
Let my people go.

They journeyed on at his command,
Let my people go;
And came at length to Canaan's land,
Let my people go.

Oh let us all from bondage flee,
Let my people go;
And let us all in Christ be free,
Let my people go.

Traditional

It is difficult to argue with those who say that Moses is the central figure in the Old Testament. Moses encounters God, is transformed by God, leads the people out of Egypt, leads them through the desert, and receives the Ten Commandments. Whatever we say about Moses, he stands as one of the most obedient figures in the Bible.

But Moses' obedience was tested from the start. "Go down, Moses, way down in Egypt's land / Tell old Pharaoh to let my people go." When Moses heard words similar to this coming from a burning bush, his first response was fearful. Meeting God in prayer is one thing, but experiencing a fiery theophany of God is another thing. It took Moses a lot of serious courage to take up God's challenge to go back to Egypt to meet the Pharaoh on his turf. But Moses did it!

To hear God's word is the first step. We are called to carry it out. To hear the call for liberation is one thing. But if we do not stand before the powers of this world and proclaim it, we fail to seek God's justice.

We sometimes forget that the final release of the Israelites took a long time. Pharaoh did not want to let the Israelites go. Like Pharaoh, we find it difficult to let go of our trappings and possessions.

"Oh let us all from bondage flee," say the words of the song. What keeps you in bondage? How can we flee from the things that trap us? This spiritual lays out the choices. Will we be Moses? Will we be Pharaoh? Will we be the Israelites on the journey?

In Moses, we have a powerful reminder that we, too, stand on holy ground and are called to participate in the ongoing acts of redemption.

Spiritual Exercise

Take off your shoes and repeat these words: "This is holy ground, I am standing on holy ground. The Lord God is here." On the second repetition, open your hands to the heavens.

Make an attempt to repeat these lines at your work, church, or in the rooms throughout your house. Just take off your shoes and repeat the words.

- What makes a place holy?

- Where do you imagine God would send Moses today? Who in today's world is Moses? Who is Pharaoh?

- Remember that the presence of God can make any ground a holy ground for you.

| THE FOURTH SUNDAY IN LENT

We Shall Overcome

We shall overcome,
We shall overcome,
We shall overcome someday;
Oh, deep in my heart,
I do believe,
We shall overcome, someday.

We'll walk hand in hand,
We'll walk hand in hand,
We'll walk hand in hand, someday;
Oh, deep in my heart,
I do believe,
We'll walk hand in hand, someday.

God is on our side,
God is on our side,
God is on our side, today;
Oh, deep in my heart,
I do believe,
God is on our side, today.

Traditional

Most of us are familiar with this song, which became popular to open and close gatherings of those fighting for racial justice and equality. In the 1950s and 1960s, those advocating for equal rights and justice chose the spirituals as their anthems. Those people who challenged the religious and political structures saw themselves as continuing a battle for freedom started by their ancestors during slavery.

"We shall overcome!" reminds us that our struggles for justice and freedom must be fought every day and in every generation. Our personal struggles for freedom and new life require daily commitments. We are never converted once and for all and forever, nor is justice ever completely won. Reality reminds us that, unfortunately, we never fully overcome. Each day presents us with the new challenge to work for justice, freedom, truth, and equality.

As Christians, we believe that we can overcome. When we struggle to overcome evil, sin, or old ways of being, we sometimes have to redefine victory. Sometimes our victories will be small and slow, but we must notice and celebrate them. Celebrating the small victories helps us to commit to larger battles.

Racism is not over in our nation, and throughout the world people are oppressed and persecuted. We must remember that God is at work. In addition, it is very important that God is calling us, like Martin Luther King Jr., to be a "drum major for justice."

Spiritual Exercise

Read John 9:1-17. Ask the Lord to reveal something special to you today.

If you attended worship today, write a poem or a letter to Jesus that best sums up your reaction to something you heard or sang or saw.

If you like to draw, draw something that represents your understanding of victory for God's people.

Reread the spiritual slowly and let it touch you deep in your heart.

■ What do you struggle to overcome in your life? What does society need to overcome?

■ What do you hold deep in your heart?

■ Remember that Jesus has overcome the world.

DAY **23** | MONDAY

Someday

Someday,
Someday
I'll go where Jesus is.
Someday, someday
I'll go where Jesus is.
Someday, someday
I'll go where Jesus is.
I'll be called out to meet Him,
Called out to meet Him where He is.

Someday,
Someday
I'll go where Jesus lives.
Someday, someday
I'll go where Jesus lives.
Someday, someday
I'll go where Jesus lives.
I'll be called out to meet Him,
Called out to meet Him where He lives.

Jamaican Traditional

"Someday I will be. . . . " "Someday I will do. . . . " So much of who we are as human beings is connected to what we will do, be, and have someday. Once while visiting a church community in Guyana, a youth stood up and prayed, "Lord, help this community to see that the youth of this church and nation are not just the future, but the present."

Whenever we think of "someday," we should try to root our wishes and hopes in the present. In this spiritual, the hope is to go where Jesus is and where Jesus lives. May we experience Jesus with us now, living in our hearts, home, church, and nation. Jesus promised to be with us always and to make his home in us.

Maybe the slaves found it hard to imagine that Jesus was with them. At times, we find it extremely difficult to believe that Jesus is with us and lives with us in the best and worst of times.

The importance of prayer lies in the ability of the person who prays to own the presence and activity of God. If our hearts are alive with a desire to experience God, we will. Saint Paul said that all he wanted in life was to know Christ and the power of his resurrection. What Paul wanted, like us, was to know in the present what he anticipated more fully in the future.

Spiritual Exercise

Find a quiet spot and think about this phrase from the spiritual: "Someday, I'll go where Jesus is. I'll be called out to meet Him." Is meeting Jesus something you fear? Look forward to? Long for? Why?

Take a few moments to reflect on Psalm 62. Read it slowly and then ask for the grace to want what Jesus wants of you.

■ What do you seek from Jesus today?

■ Where do you see yourself in your faith journey tomorrow, next week, next year?

■ Remember that Jesus wants to be with you today.

DAY **24** | **TUESDAY**

King Jesus Is A-Listenin'

King Jesus is a listenin' all day long,
King Jesus is a listenin' all day long,
King Jesus is a listenin' all day long,
To hear some sinner pray.

That Gospel train is comin',
A rumblin through the lan',
But I hear the wheels a hummin',
Get ready to board that train.

I know I been converted,
I ain't gon' make no alarm,
For my soul is bound for glory,
And the devil can't do me no harm.

Traditional

I once asked a psychologist what plagues the human person more than anything else. He said, "People hurt the most when they don't feel listened to by others." If we stop and think, we would realize that we are at our best when we feel listened to by those closest to us. Children often complain that their parents do not listen to them, and spouses have the same complaint about their partners.

The singers of this spiritual felt tremendous pain, both physically and emotionally. The system of slavery not only robbed them of home, family, and loved ones but made them subhuman. Dogs and cats were shown more attention and given more care than the slaves. Slaves had no voice. They were separated from those who spoke their language, separated from families and members of their tribe. This further deprived them of a voice. Imagine the agony they must have endured.

In Brazil, many of the slaves were baptized and given membership in churches. These slaves, and others throughout the Americas, were allowed to attend church services—yet they were segregated and not allowed to participate or pray aloud. The more the slaves learned about God, the more they came to an awareness that God was listening to them. This is a delightful song, in the way it shows the theological development of the slaves and the aspects of scripture they considered important.

The singers of this spiritual knew without a doubt that "King Jesus is a listenin' all day long." There is an old African proverb that says, "The gods will come when you sing them a song." Imagine the faith of these slaves who believed that Jesus was listening to them and would come to their aid. "The devil can't do me no harm," runs another line. Slavery inflicted many harms, but the slaves came to a terrific understanding of what Jesus meant when he said, "Fear not those who harm the body."

When we listen to each other, we imitate the presence of Jesus in this world. May this spiritual remind us of the importance of listening to the voices of others, especially the poor, the weak, and the young.

Spiritual Exercise

Spend time today being aware of the presence of Jesus. Light a candle or look at a crucifix or a cross and simply ask Jesus to draw close to you. Imagine that Jesus is pouring blessings unto your life and into your heart. You might imagine that you are an empty vessel being filled with God's love and blessings.

Now bring to mind those who refuse to acknowledge your voice. Imagine that one by one they stand before you. Call their names and see them come toward you. Now place your hand on their head and pray for them. See the blessing and forgiveness of God pouring out of you upon them. Do this for each person.

Repeat these words before going to bed: "King Jesus is a listenin' all day long / To hear some sinner pray."

- Why do you find it difficult to listen to others?

- What happens to a person when he or she does not have a voice, does not feel listened to by others?

- Remember Jesus wants to hear what you have to say. What do you have to say to Jesus?

DAY **25** | WEDNESDAY

He Is King of Kings

He is King of kings,
He is Lord of lords;
Jesus Christ, the first and last
No man works like Him.

He built his throne up in the air,
No man works like Him;
And called the saints from everywhere,
No man works like Him.

I was but young when I begun,
No man works like Him;
But now my race is almost won,
No man works like Him.

Traditional

In the incarnation, God becomes human. God chose to identify with us. Because of this mystery, we can identify more easily with God. The more we see our lives mirrored in Jesus and Jesus' life mirrored in us, the more we approximate the true meaning and purpose of life.

"No man works like Him" could well have been a spiritual song by the slaves to console each other. So great was their identification with Jesus. Although their life of pain and suffering was hard, they believed it was harder for Jesus. An insight such as this is quite powerful and important. We sometimes forget the reality of Jesus' life. He was born next to animals, walked the streets, was homeless, was rejected and betrayed, and died a horrible death. Our pictures and stories oftentimes portray a more appealing Jesus, but that is not the case.

The more we see the Gospels and Jesus in their reality the more mercy and compassion we will have toward those who suffer. "No man works like Him" could become "No one suffers like Him."

Whenever my mother saw us feeling sorry for ourselves, she would say, "There is someone out there suffering more than you." That did not console us most times, but it was true. Once I told a nun that I was feeling a sharp pain in my arm. "Offer it up to sweet Jesus," she said. This was her way of reminding me that in suffering, I could and should make a connection to Jesus.

As Christians, we are called to connect our lives to Jesus. Unfortunately, we sometimes feel that God does not want to hear about our work, our suffering, our doubts, and our pain. When we acknowledge that Jesus experienced the same, it may be easier to pray through the rough times.

Spiritual Exercise

Find a crucifix or a cross and go to a quiet spot. Talk to Jesus on the cross or invent a dialogue with the cross.

Recite these lines slowly and lovingly, pausing every now and then. "He is King of kings /He is Lord of lords / Jesus Christ, the first and last."

Then spend a few moments reflecting on the events of your life since Ash Wednesday. Use this phrase to give thanks for all the events that have happened in your life so far. Pray a blessing for the people you have met, for the people you work with, and for those you live with. When you have finished, imagine that you are pouring these words of blessing on the heads of those you ask a blessing.

- What does it mean to have Jesus as Lord of your life?

- What blessings do you want God to pour on your head?

- Remember that you are a work in progress.

DAY **26** | THURSDAY

Babylon, Yuh Throne Gaan Down

Babylon, you gone down;
Oppressor man, you gone down.
Oppressor man, you gone;
Babylon, you gone;
An' yuh throne gaan down.

Jamaican Traditional

Jamaicans use the term "Babylon" to refer to any system or culture that causes oppression or suffering. During the 1960s, the Rastafarian movement continued its call for Jamaicans to look toward Africa and to leave Babylon. Interestingly enough, while the slaves sang about the defeat of Babylon, the late twentieth-century members of the Rastafarian movement sang about "chanting down and out Babylon."

A famous saying goes like this: "The more things change the more they remain the same." In talking about sin, novelist Graham Greene says that it is impossible for humans to invent a new sin. We are often faced with the recurrence of evil and the need to be vigilant in the face of evil and sin.

What the singers of this Jamaican spiritual offered was a faith in good over evil. As Christians we are called to celebrate the victory of life over death and righteousness over sin. Throughout our lives we live the tension of the now and the not yet. Salvation is present, but not in its fullness. To ensure the salvation of God in today's world and in our lives, we are called to practice a faith that is committed and vigilant.

It must have been hard for the slaves to sing about victory even as they were oppressed, but this is the great lesson they offer us in this season of Lent. The battle has already been won. Babylon has indeed fallen. To live this reality requires that we remain vigilant and employ the necessary tools to ensure that our good is never overcome by evil. The light of Christ in our hearts must never be overcome by darkness. This is our challenge.

Spiritual Exercise

Read John 1:1-18. Take a word or a phrase and let it echo through your heart and mind. You may take the phrase "in the beginning was the Word." Or you might choose "the Word became flesh and dwelt among us." Or you might find it useful to reflect on the theme of light and darkness.

Read this rich passage a few times during the day. You will find that it will help your understanding of Jesus' mission and will enrich your meditation on "Babylon."

■ What does it mean for you to believe that "Babylon" is defeated? How do you understand the phrase "and darkness did not overcome the light"?

■ What are the structures that promote evil in our society and world? How do you contribute to sin and evil?

■ Remember that Jesus was tempted by the forces of evil.

DAY **27** | FRIDAY

Done Made My Vow

Done made my vow to the Lord,
And I never will turn back,
Oh I will go, I shall go
To see what the end will be.

Sometimes I'm up, sometimes I'm down;
See what the end will be,
But still my soul was heav'nly bound,
See what the end will be.

When I was a mourner just like you;
See what the end will be,
I prayed and prayed 'til I came through,
See what the end will be.

Traditional

There have been many concerns about the ability of this generation of young people to commit to anything. Sometimes we project our failings unto others as a way of dealing with our shortcomings. I, for one, do not believe that this generation of young people is less committed than any other generation has been. Whatever the case is, there is no denying that we are called to remain faithful to our vows, promises, and words.

"Done made my vow to the Lord / And I never will turn back / Oh I will go, I shall go / To see what the end will be" goes this spiritual. During Lent, we meditate and pay attention because we want "to see what the end will be." We may recall the experience of two of the first disciples of Jesus. They wanted to learn more about him and he invited them to come and see.

There is no mention of how long it took them to get to Jesus' place of rest. I suspect that this was the Evangelist's way of saying that those who follow Jesus must follow him to the end. Following Jesus does require a commitment to remaining on the path. Buddhists say that staying on the path means following the instruction to stay on the path. To see the end, you must desire to see the end. Whether you are young or old, it is not a question of who is more committed, but more a question of how we can help each other to get to the end of the narrow road.

During Lent, we have a wonderful opportunity to imitate Jesus who turned his face toward Jerusalem and "prayed and prayed" until he came through. In obedience to God, Jesus gave his life up to the end, and beyond.

Spiritual Exercise

Spend some reading the responses Jesus made during his temptation in Matthew 4:1-11. They are based on Deuteronomy 8:3; 6:16; 6:13; and Psalm 91:11-12.

Write down these responses and put them on a place you know you will see them. Try to memorize them.

Spend some time with these lines from the spiritual: "Sometimes I'm up, sometimes I'm down / See what the end will be / But still my soul was heav'nly bound / See what the end will be."

What is "the end" in this spiritual?

■ Who encourages you on your journey of faith? What helps you to persevere?

■ What temptations have you been facing lately? What is the Lord teaching you?

■ Remember that Jesus experienced more temptations even while nailed to the cross.

DAY **28** | SATURDAY

Sometimes I Feel Like a Motherless Chile

Sometimes I feel like a motherless chile,
Sometimes I feel like a motherless chile,
Sometimes I feel like a motherless chile,
A long ways from home,
A long ways from home.
Then I get down on my knees an' pray,
Get down on my knees and pray.

Sometimes I feel like I'm almos' gone,
Sometimes I feel like I'm almos' gone,
Sometimes I feel like I'm almos' gone,
A long ways from home,
A long ways from home.
Then I get down on my knees an' pray,
Get down on my knees an' pray.

Traditional

Loneliness can be a most painful emotion. I once knew a priest who had a nervous breakdown. What surprised me about this was that he was quite popular and well-liked. People thought he was the most integrated human being. A few days before his breakdown, he came to visit me. For some reason, we seemed to be talking about inconsequential things. After a while, he burst into tears and said, "With all these people who love me, I feel so lonely, so alone."

So many of us struggle with feelings of loneliness. Sometimes these feelings lead us into many destructive patterns. One of the most powerful questions I have ever been asked was this: How do I deal with loneliness? It is an important question for us to ask and to answer every so often in our lives.

Compassion means the ability to feel. If we reach out to others when we are feeling lonely or alone, we might well find the friend we need. In this spiritual, we get a glimpse of the intense loneliness the slaves must have felt. "Sometimes I feel like a motherless chile / Sometimes I feel like I'm almost gone." Of course, many slaves were separated from mother and father, sister and brother. To "feel like a motherless child" must be the most painful and lonely of situations.

If Jesus says woe to those who scandalize children, imagine what he would say to those who cause a child to be motherless. We must weep for the sin of a society and Christianity that condoned slavery. And when we have wept, we must work to fight against all systems of oppression that leave children motherless.

Transforming our feelings of loneliness into acts of compassion and advocacy can bring about the healing we need in our lives.

Spiritual Exercise

Try fasting today. When we fast, we get in touch with our uncontrolled desires and gain control and understanding of them. Try skipping lunch or dinner. When you begin fasting it is important not to be too drastic, but begin slowly by giving up a meal. While fasting, it is important to drink plenty of water or fruit juice.

As you fast, place yourself next to Jesus in the desert. Identify with his sense of being alone and lonely.

Abstinence and sacrifice get a bad rap in today's culture, but there is merit in each of them. Try abstaining from something you like and spend that time in prayer.

■ When have you been most lonely?

■ Have you ever felt like a motherless child? Do you know someone who is lonely? What can you to do be present to that person?

■ Remember that whatever you do to the "least," you do to Jesus.

Come by Here

Come by here, Lord,
Come by here,
Come by here, Lord,
Come by here,
Come by here, Lord,
Come by here.
O Lord,
Come by here.

Someone needs you, Lord,
Come by here,
Someone needs you, Lord,
Come by here,
Someone needs you, Lord,
Come by here.
O Lord,
Come by here.

Someone's crying, Lord,
Come by here,
Someone's crying Lord,
Come by here,
Someone's crying Lord,
Come by here.
O Lord,
Come by here.

Traditional

In this translation of "Kumbaya, mah Lawd" the singers call out to God to come by and be a part of what they are experiencing. The sentiments are simply expressed, but they touch all human hearts in a gentle, but powerful, way.

In our pride, we tend to invite people to our home only when it is clean or we have something new to show them. Imagine the confidence the slaves must have had in Jesus to want Jesus to come and be a part of their experience. Those with eyes of faith must have often seen "One like the Son of Man" working in the cane fields along with the slaves. Yes, if we invite Jesus, he does come.

To desire that Jesus come into our hearts and the situations of our lives is the greatest thing we can do as Christians. One of our greatest gifts is freedom. We have the freedom to invite or reject God. Since God gave us the gift of freedom, God respects our choices. Imagine the power in our hands, a power to call God to be a part of our life, to be a part of our suffering and to be a part of our joys. "Someone's crying Lord / Come by here." Personally, I do not think there is a more beautiful prayer.

Spiritual Exercise

If you do this meditation before you go to church, ask God to "come by" your house or whatever situation you may be facing in your life. Just repeat these words: "Come by here, Lord." Repeat them slowly and lovingly, placing your right hand over your heart.

If you went to church today, try to recapture what was said in the homily or one of the readings you heard in church. Try listing three points from the readings or homily. For those who did not get to attend church, read John 12:1-8.

- Into which situation in your life or in the life of some family member would you like to invite Jesus?

- Where is God, your church community, or the needs of the world inviting you?

- Remember that if you call on God, God will answer.

DAY **29** | MONDAY

Rockin' Jerusalem

O Mary, O Martha, O Mary, ring dem bells.
O Mary, O Martha, O Mary, ring dem bells.
I hear archangels a rockin' in Jerusalem,
I hear archangels a ringin' dem bells.

Church gettin' higher! Rockin' Jerusalem!
Church gettin' higher! ringin' dem bells.

New Jerusalem! Rockin' Jerusalem!
New Jerusalem ringin' dem bells.

Traditional

M ary and Martha were two of Jesus' closest friends. They opened their home to Jesus, and he found solace in their friendship. Both women offer us a chance to examine our posture before God. They offer us a look at humanity's greatest challenge—doing or being.

Martha was interested in cooking and doing other chores as part of welcoming Jesus. She tried to be the perfect host. Much can be said for Martha's focus on hospitality, on making visitors such as Jesus welcome in her home.

Mary, on the other hand, wanted to be with Jesus. She wanted to sit at the feet of her master and listen and learn. Did that make Mary a slacker? Martha seemed to think that Mary wasn't carrying her weight. Martha was so angry that she did not even address her sister. Instead, she spoke directly to Jesus. How embarrassing for Mary. If Martha thought she could embarrass Jesus into sending Mary away, she was wrong. Jesus acknowledged the need for disciples to sit at his feet and listen, even if others had justifiable demands on their time.

Of course, when we pray we could well be doing something else. When we do acts of charity, we could be doing something else. When we spend time relaxing, we could be doing work. These women offer us an insight into the human condition and God's wisdom.

Worrying has its place, but fussing about in the name of being hospitable is never more important than being a disciple. True worship, sitting at Jesus' feet, is what Mary chose and so Jesus assigns to her the task of the archangels. She rings the bell.

The slaves must have heard the church bells many times. Some were forced to attend church, but they made the distinction between the church of the slaveholders and the church of the New Jerusalem.

Our prayers and time spent with Jesus will be greatly rewarded.

Spiritual Exercise

Try to block three ten-minute slots in your day today. You might want to plan your reflection time to coincide with some activity you need to do. Make a conscious decision to take a ten-minute break and be aware of God's presence.

Holy men and women throughout the ages have encouraged us to pray constantly. No one has ever said we should work all the time. Ignatius of Loyola said that it is important that we find God in all things. So stop working and turn your eyes to the face of Jesus. Stop your doing and just be present to Jesus.

Sit and be still. Do not say anything or think anything; just make the effort to know that you are in the presence of God and that God wants to honor your efforts to be with Jesus.

- How do you live out your Christian commitment in your work? How do you find God in all things?

- What does the concept of the Sabbath or the Lord's Day mean for you? How is this lived out on a daily basis?

- Remember that Jesus said of Mary's decision to sit in his presence, "Mary, has chosen the better part and it will not be taken from her."

DAY **30** | TUESDAY

Oh, Mary, Don't You Weep, Don't You Mourn

Oh Mary, don't you weep, don't you mourn,
Oh Mary, don't you weep, don't you mourn.
Pharaoh's army got drowned,
Oh Mary, don't you weep.

Some of these mornings bright and fair,
Take my wings and cleave the air.
Pharaoh's army got drowned,
Oh Mary, don't you weep.

When I get to heaven goin' to sing and shout,
Nobody there for to turn me out.
Pharaoh's army got drowned,
Oh Mary, don't you weep.

When I get to heaven goin' to put on my shoes,
Run about Glory and tell all the news.
Pharaoh's army got drowned,
Oh Mary, don't you weep.

Traditional

Imitating someone's good actions is the best compliment we can give another person. Jesus said, "Be perfect, as your heavenly Father is perfect!" Well, that is impossible, but we can certainly make it our goal. If we cannot always imitate the good in others, we can at least try to identify with their goodness, their pain, or their dreams.

Much of what we do in spiritual meditation is to identify with Jesus and others in the Bible as a means to imitate them. In many ways, it would help if we saw the incarnation of Jesus as God identifying with us.

This spiritual gives an example of the slaves identifying with Mary. The Virgin Mary has many titles in the Roman Catholic tradition. One of her most famous and endearing titles is Our Lady of Sorrows. The slaves came to identify with Mary's sorrow and tremendous sense of loss as she watched her son Jesus crucified to death.

But their knowledge of the faith leads them to console Mary. Their knowledge of the Bible and suffering leads them to remind Mary that "Pharaoh's army got drowned."

The jaws of death may seem to catch us and be ready to devour us, but God will drown our enemies and the things that seek to destroy us. But the slaves have a tremendous sense of reality. Their faith gives them hope in the present, but they know that only in heaven will things be right and fair. "When I get to heaven goin' to sing and shout / Nobody there for to turn me out / Pharaoh's army got drowned / Oh Mary, don't you weep."

"Don't you weep" does not tell us that pain will not happen in life. It reminds us that in our darkest hour there is hope.

Bob Marley responded to this spiritual with a reggae anthem that says, "No woman, no cry." Do not cry for too long, women. Do not cry for too long, my people. Remember that God has defeated evil, sin, guilt, and shame.

Spiritual Exercise

Mary stands as an important person in our salvation history, and undeniably in the life of Jesus. We can respect her place in the life of Jesus without taking away the glory and honor due to Jesus.

Take a few moments to reflect on Mary in chapters 1 and 2 of Luke, especially Luke 1:26-56 and 2:32-52. Look at her posture of listening to God and try to identify with her feelings of joy and pain. Allow her words to become yours.

Try to have a dialogue with Mary and ask her to tell you about her Son. Most mothers love to talk about their children, and I am sure Mary is no exception.

Spend time with Mary and see what happens.

- What does Mary's silence teach us? What about Mary appeals to you?

- What do the words "don't you weep" mean to you? When was the last time you wept?

- Remember that Jesus wept at the death of his friend Lazarus.

DAY **31** | WEDNESDAY

Do Lord, Remember Me

Do Lord, do Lord,
Do remember me,
Do Lord, do Lord,
Do remember me,
Do Lord, do Lord,
Do remember me.
Look away beyond the blue.

When I'm in trouble,
Do remember me,
When I'm in trouble,
Do remember me,
When I'm in trouble,
Do remember me.
Look away beyond the blue.

I've got a home in glory land
That outshines the sun;
I've got a home in glory land
That outshines the sun;
I've got a home in glory land
That outshines the sun.
Look away beyond the blue.

Traditional

If you work in a business in Jamaica, the words you do not want to hear are "Do you remember me?" I like to walk up to important people in Jamaica and ask that question. To remember in Jamaica is to have an obligation. If I remember that you were kind to me, I am obligated to return the favor. "Do you remember me?" can also be a way of saying, "You did not fulfill my wishes the last time."

Life happens so quickly that most of us can hardly remember what happened yesterday, much less ten years ago. Yet if we spend the time to watch the news or read the newspaper, we realize that scientists are making findings about the world millions of years ago. Individually, it is easy to forget, but more and more the collective consciousness of groups reminds us of the importance of remembering.

Every Sunday we remember how Jesus loved us and we celebrate that love, knowing he is with us. In truth, Jesus told us to come together and break the bread and drink the wine in memory of him. Every eucharist is an act of remembering, but also a call to Jesus to "remember me."

This spiritual reminds us that we should never forget the words of Jesus to store up for ourselves treasures in heaven. From the cruelty of slavery, the slaves looked up and saw the glory of God, "that outshines the sun." This gave them confidence and gives us the confidence to pray, "When I'm in trouble / Do remember me / Look away beyond the blue."

Spiritual Exercise

Spend some time repeating the following words: "While they were at supper . . . he took the bread . . . said a blessing . . . broke the bread . . . gave it to his disciples and said . . . 'Take this all of you . . . and eat it . . . this is my body . . . which will be given up for you. . . . Do this . . . in memory of me.'"

Then at another time in the day repeat these words: "When supper was ended . . . he took the cup . . . said a blessing . . . gave it to his disciples and said . . . 'Take this all of you . . . and drink of it . . . this is the blood of the new and everlasting covenant . . . it will be shed for you . . . and for all people. . . . Do this . . . in memory of me.'"

As you repeat this throughout the day, spend time with the word or the phrase that touches your heart.

- What do you remember about your earliest days in church? What memories do have of your childhood church?

- What does Jesus remember about you? What passage from the Bible comes most easily to your mind?

- Remember that you are an earthen vessel with wealth untold.

DAY **32** | **THURSDAY**

Nobody Knows the Trouble I've Seen

Nobody knows the trouble I've seen, Lord,
Nobody knows but Jesus.
Nobody knows the trouble I've seen,
Glory, hallelujah.

Sometimes I'm up, sometimes I'm down, Oh, yes, Lord,
Sometimes I'm almost to the ground,
Oh, yes, Lord.

Although you see me going 'long so, Oh yes, Lord,
I have my troubles here below,
Oh, yes, Lord.

Traditional

Nobody knows us. Nobody really understands us. Sometimes we can feel this way—unknown and misunderstood. But Jesus knows us. What relief to remember that Jesus always knows. He really knows us. And that should bring us a lot of consolation. Beyond our defenses, beyond all the masks we wear to survive in this rough world, Jesus is there, exquisitely attuned to who we really are.

Sometimes our pain drives us inward, preventing others from getting to know us. We can focus so intently on our pain that we separate ourselves from community. "Leave me alone, you can never understand my pain," we sometimes say. If we imagine, for example, that nobody suffers like we do, we may fall into the trap of living independently of others.

Nelson Mandela often warned other South Africans not to become like oppressors. If we cling to pain and suffering in a destructive manner, when life gives us the upper hand we may be inclined to inflict pain on others.

"Nobody knows the trouble I've seen." While it is true that no one will experience our pain or suffering just as we do, it is not true that nobody knows. Those people whom we allow to share our love and pain, they know because our trouble resonates with them.

This awareness of shared pain and the accompaniment of Jesus in all our troubles and suffering helps us to move from our lonely, separated selves toward real communion. Because Jesus knows our suffering, because all people know suffering, we can make space to receive support and we can help others to share their pain, confident that we will not abandon them.

Spiritual Exercise

Try to be aware of how your home, church, and community supports the suffering and pain of others. Start by asking yourself this question, "What do I do that causes others to suffer?"

Repeat these lines: "O, my God, I am truly sorry for having offended you and I detest all that I have done to cause pain and suffering in others."

Say the Lord's Prayer slowly and lovingly.

■ What suffering exists in your family that you have ignored or hidden from consciousness? What pain do you cause others?

■ How do people around you hide their pain? Why? How do others know when you are suffering?

■ Remember that Jesus knows your suffering and pain.

DAY **33** | **FRIDAY**

Amen

Amen, amen, amen, amen, amen.

See the little baby
Lying in a manger
On Christmas morning.

See Him in the temple
Talking to the elders;
They marv'led at His wisdom.

See him in the garden
Praying to His Father
As Judas betrays Him.

See Him there at Calvary
Dying for us sinners,
But He rose on Easter.

Traditional

The metaphysical poets of the sixteenth century developed a theme they labeled "from the cradle to the grave." Salvation history, in their view, began with the birth of Christ in a manger and got mirrored in the experience of Jesus' death. When we read the Christmas stories, we see hints of Jesus' impending suffering. He was born on the outskirts of society and he died in like manner. He was born in a manger and buried in a tomb that did not belong to his family. The gifts of the magi must have left his parents wondering about the fate of their child.

There is no denying that death is a companion of life. Every new experience of life is couched in death. We grow because our cells die and give birth to new ones. How wonderful our lives would be if we could embrace the mystery of death all around us, and see it as the gateway to new life.

In the movie *Moonstruck*, one of the characters asked why men cheat on their wives. There were other answers given, but the correct answer was that men were afraid to die. Fear of death prevents us from experiencing life in its fullness.

"See the little baby . . ." moves to "see Him there at Calvary." What a powerful connection the slaves made for all of us. If we can see the child in each person we meet, we may treat them differently. This spiritual stood as a creed for the slaves, reminding us that the most profound things in life can be said in simple ways.

We do not need to complicate our lives any further. All we need to do is realize that life is a gift—all of it. This gift of life has death as an important component, a death that leads to Easter. Let us not be afraid, because Jesus has conquered death.

Spiritual Exercise

Imagine that you see your body laid out in church for the funeral services. Take a good look at your body. Notice what you are wearing. Pay special attention to the look or expression on your face.

Look at the people who come to pay their respects and to say good-bye. What would you like to say to them?

Try to hear what they are saying. See whether you can notice what they are feeling and doing. What hymns are played? What Bible passages are read? Who is preaching? What are the words of the homily?

Speak to Jesus about the emotions this exercise brought up for you. If you find this exercise difficult, talk honestly to Jesus about it.

- If you were to die today, would you be ready? Ready for what?

- What experiences in your childhood or in your family would you change if you could? What changes in your life would you make to prepare for death?

- Remember that death is inevitable and that it paves the way for a new life in God.

DAY **34** | SATURDAY

Ride on, King Jesus

Ride on, King Jesus,
No man can hinder me.
Ride on, King Jesus, ride on,
No man can hinder me.

King Jesus rides a milk-white horse,
No man works like Him.
De river Jordan He did cross,
No man works like Him.

I know that my redeemer lives,
No man works like Him.
And of His blessing freely gives,
No man works like Him.

Traditional

"Ride on, King Jesus / No man can hinder me." There is a chorus that says, "In the name of Jesus, we have the victory." As Christians, for us to live is to believe in Jesus. We believe that as long as Jesus is riding ahead of us, things will work out all right. This experience was lived out and modeled by the Israelites in the desert, by Job in the midst of his afflictions and by the slaves. To believe in ultimate victory is to stand undefeated by the disappointments, frustrations, and the setbacks of life.

We sometimes forget that God works. We forget that God's creation continues to unfold and that we are called to labor in the vineyard of God. "No man works like Him" is a true statement and it brings us a lot of consolation. What would be depressing to hear is that no one is working with Jesus or for Jesus. When we think of God as riding and working on, we are reminded that we need to do our part.

God needs us, and the scriptures remind us constantly that Jesus sent out his disciples to work for the reign of God. Our redeemer lives and there is hope. What a great opportunity we have in this season of Lent to reflect on the ongoing work of God. We cannot be hindered and must not hinder others in the work of the kingdom. Let us ride on with Jesus; let us go to Jerusalem with him. Let us stay with him and work with him. Let us ride on.

Spiritual Exercise

Sit still and be aware that you are in God's presence. Think about offering all that you have and are to Jesus. Say, "Jesus, take my lips . . . my ears . . . my thoughts . . . my hands. . . ." As you offer your whole body to the Lord, touch these places or raise them up as a sign of offering all that you are to Jesus.

Make a promise today to say "Thank you," "I love you," and "I am sorry" to the appropriate people.

At the end of the day, ask the Lord for the grace to enter into Holy Week with a heart committed to work for him.

- Why do you ride with Jesus? What has that ride been like for you?

- What have you done for Jesus? What are you doing for Jesus? What do you need to keep doing for Jesus?

- Remember that Jesus will never give up on you.

THE SIXTH SUNDAY IN LENT
PALM SUNDAY / PASSION SUNDAY

Lord, I Want to Be a Christian

Lord, I want to be a Christian in my heart, in my heart,
Lord, I want to be a Christian in my heart.

In my heart, in my heart,
Lord, I want to be a Christian in my heart.

Lord, I want to be more loving in my heart, in my heart,
Lord, I want to be more loving in my heart.

Lord, I want to be more holy, in my heart,
Lord, I want to be more holy, in my heart.

Lord, I don't want to be like Judas, in my heart, in my heart,
Lord, I don't want to be like Judas, in my heart.

Lord, I want to be like Jesus, in my heart, in my heart,
Lord, I want to be like Jesus, in my heart.

Traditional

Palm Sunday, also called Passion Sunday, brings a new energy to our walk during Lent. All the readings present a theology of suffering and redemption. We are called to find God in the suffering servant described in Isaiah and to relive with Jesus all the painful events that led up to his death.

In a strange way, Palm Sunday calls us into the future. The palms we wave today will be the ashes for next Ash Wednesday. An exuberant crowd soon becomes a crowd that rejects Jesus' message as too revolutionary. Once again, the theme of life and death is present to us. When we wave the palms, we should ask ourselves how seriously we take our commitment to Jesus.

Few of us would identify with Judas, Peter, the bloodthirsty and mocking crowds, Pilate, or the Roman soldiers. But all of us have had moments when we have denied, betrayed, and walked away from Jesus. Palm Sunday calls us to recognize what is real and truthful. We are called to know where we stand in the march to Calvary.

The story of the passion of Jesus is a story rich in emotion. We stand witness to God being rejected, beaten, and executed. Where are we in this story? How does the passion of Jesus get lived out in today's world?

In the midst of all the rejection, pain, and suffering that Jesus experiences, his posture is one of humility and compassionate actions. Over and over again, he extends a hand of healing, compassion, and forgiveness to those who hurt him.

It is easy for us to justify the pain we suffer and to justify our desire for revenge or what we call justice. If Palm Sunday teaches us anything, it is caution. We need to be careful how we join the voices of those who wish to justify killing, justify cutting off aid to the poor, and justify war.

This spiritual gives the best advice as to what our posture should be on Palm Sunday and all our lives: "Lord, I want to be like Jesus, in my heart." To desire to be like Jesus in our heart, the deepest part of our being, is the greatest posture we can take before God.

To take on the posture of Jesus Christ in all that we do and say requires God's grace, constant prayer, and vigilant faith.

Spiritual Exercise

Read Luke 23:1–49. Choose a disciple to identify with and imagine a scene where you are that disciple. What are you thinking about Jesus' words? Where are you as Jesus makes his triumphant entry into Jerusalem? Try making eye contact with Jesus. What is it like to look into Jesus' eyes as he prepares for suffering?

Imagine that you get a few moments to be alone with Jesus today, repeat the words of the spiritual to him: "Lord, I want to be a Christian in my heart . . . Lord I want to be like you in my heart."

- Why are the crowds determined to crucify Jesus? What has Jesus done to deserve this treatment?

- What does it mean for Jesus to be the Suffering Servant? If you met Jesus in the midst of his suffering, what would be your reaction?

- Remember that the passion of Jesus is being lived out today in the lives of many people.

- Remember that Jesus calls you to go against the wishes and cries of the multitude and to take up your cross and follow him.

DAY **35** | MONDAY OF HOLY WEEK

At the Cross

At the cross, at the cross
Where I first saw the light,
And the burden of my heart rolled away:
It was near that cross
That I received my sight,
And now I am happy all the way.

Jamaican Traditional

The readings, the songs, the prayers, and the activities of Lent call us to the cross. "At the cross, at the cross" is where we find our light and our God. Implicit in all the readings throughout Lent is the call by Jesus to take up the cross and follow him. To be Christian is to be like Jesus, to carry the cross.

Some of us jump at the invitation to carry the cross or help carry the cross, but when the moment of crucifixion arrives, we run away. As Jesus carried the cross, the weight of it must have reminded him of what he would suffer. He must have prayed for strength and courage with every step on the way to Calvary.

Maybe Jesus thought of the bronze snake that Moses fashioned and held up, so that the Israelites bitten by poisonous snakes in the wilderness might look upon it and be healed. Perhaps Jesus saw himself as being lifted up on the cross, so that those who look on him would find life.

When we look at the lives of the saints, of Martin Luther King Jr., Nelson Mandela, Oscar Romero, Mother Teresa, and many others, we experience healing and encouragement. To look at those who embrace their cross and who are nailed to it is to find the courage to keep carrying our crosses.

The condition of slavery gave the slaves a unique perspective. They identified with Jesus, the suffering servant who died on the cross. They could identify with the passion of Jesus. This spiritual says that it was at the cross the singers first saw the light. Revelation came at the cross, because there are many lessons to learn in watching and experiencing the sufferings of others.

Many times there is not much we can do in light of suffering, but we can bring our presence, a presence that has been to the cross. Next to the bedside of a sick child or a dying relative, we can only be present. Being present teaches us what to do. We must not try to do things before being present. Today, there seems to be more emphasis on human doing than on human being.

Holy Week is a time to remember the costs of being with Jesus and sharing his suffering. We are most vulnerable when we suffer. To turn away from looking at the cross is to turn away from healing and merciful actions.

As we journey with Jesus this week, may we find the grace to be at the cross, and may we experience the light that shines from it.

Spiritual Exercise

Read Mark 15:21-32. Take a few moments and imagine what was happening at the cross and around the cross when Jesus died.

Imagine that you are at the foot of the cross looking up at Jesus. What does it feel like?

If you have access to the Stations of the Cross, you may read them and reflect on them.

Another exercise worth doing is to imagine that you are the cross of Jesus. Trace the origin of the tree. What kind of a tree do you imagine the cross was made from? Who owned this tree? What did it look like? Who prepared the wood for the cross? Who brought it in to hand to Jesus?

You might want to imagine talking to the cross or write a dialogue you think the cross would have had with Jesus.

- What cross do you bear? Who is suffering under a weight of a heavy cross in your family, church, or society?

- How do you remain present to those who suffer? How are you present to your own crosses? By engaging in the suffering of others, what lessons do you learn?

- Remember that there is a cross for everyone.

- Remember that there is always the temptation to believe our burden is the heaviest.

DAY **36** | TUESDAY OF HOLY WEEK

God Is So Good

God is so good, God is so good,
God is so good, He's so good to me.

He cares for me, He cares for me,
He cares for me, He's so good to me.

He's all I need, He's all I need,
He's all I need, He's so good to me.

Traditional

Can we believe in the goodness of God during Holy Week? Can we believe in the goodness of God in our suffering and loss?

As Holy Week continues, we pause to remember the goodness of God incarnated in the pain and suffering of Jesus, which can become too much for us to fathom and bear. When we read the Gospels, we often miss the power of the words and actions of Jesus. On close examination, we discover the radical nature and implications of what Jesus said and did.

Jesus lived a life of radical inclusivity, reaching out to all those on the margins of society. He refused to be controlled by the society's marginalized views of women and included them in his ministry. Jesus refused to stereotype others into the categories of clean and unclean.

As a Jew, Jesus did not preach that salvation was open only to the Jews but instead preached a message of salvation for all peoples. Jesus opposed all kinds of oppression. He opposed the religious oppression and hypocrisy of his day. He argued for an interpretation of the law that was based on love.

One of the most subtle but powerful messages of Jesus was the message against idolatry. Jesus worked against any belief system that caused people to abandon the God of life.

Jesus challenged the religious and political power of his day and reminded them that all power and glory belong to God. Imagine what it would mean for us to challenge the religious and political powers of our day. Imagine what would happen if we entered in our churches and turned the altar around, threw out the pews, turned off the pipe organ and had children preach. Oh yes, Jesus challenged so many of the things people treasured that he became a huge threat. He even challenged how people responded to their enemies, asking them to respond in love.

All these actions of Jesus led to a concerted commitment on the part of many to bring him to death. Seeing the death of an innocent person is quite painful, although we continue to put to death many innocent people.

But there is something so shocking about seeing a religious person, seemingly abandoned by God, being killed by seemingly religious people. We often react the way Job's friends reacted.

"Where is God, when we most need God?" God in Jesus is hanging on a cross.

In this spiritual, the singers claim the goodness of God in the depths of their pain. It is like a prisoner in the darkest dungeon hearing the song of a bird. Life goes on outside our suffering, but God exists in all our suffering. "He cares for me / He's all I need / He's so good to me."

Spiritual Exercise

Read Luke 22:39-46. Be present with Jesus as he prays in the Garden of Gethsemane. Imagine that you stay awake and watch with Jesus, even as the other disciples fall asleep. Look at the Son of God facing his fear and loneliness. Pay special attention to Jesus' face and see whether you can detect what he is feeling. Imagine that you go up to him and wipe his face or rest your hand on his shoulder.

Notice the tenderness of Jesus in this hour of crisis. Notice his faith and how he proclaims in his actions that God cares for him.

Take a few more minutes to pray for the grace to be able to proclaim the goodness of God at all times.

- When was the last time you prayed for those on death row? When was the last time you prayed for those at risk of betrayal and violence?

- How do you remind others of God's love and constancy? Where do you find evidence of the goodness of God in your life?

- Remember that God's angels are watching over you and that in the end all things will be well.

DAY **37** | WEDNESDAY OF HOLY WEEK

Hush, Hush, Somebody's Callin' My Name

Hush, hush, somebody's callin' my name.
Hush, hush, somebody's callin' my name.
Hush, hush, somebody's callin' my name.
Oh my Lord, Oh my Lord,
What shall I do? What shall I do?

Sounds like Jesus, somebody's calling my name.
Sounds like Jesus, somebody's calling my name.
Sounds like Jesus, somebody's calling my name.
Oh my Lord, Oh my Lord,
What shall I do? What shall I do?

Soon one mornin' death'll come creepin' in my room.
Soon one mornin' death'll come creepin' in my room.
Soon one mornin' death'll come creepin' in my room.
Oh my Lord, Oh my Lord,
What shall I do? What shall I do?

I'm so glad, I got my religion in time.
I'm so glad, I got my religion in time.
I'm so glad, I got my religion in time.
Oh my Lord, Oh my Lord,
What shall I do? What shall I do?

Traditional

The Wednesday of Holy Week is a very special time, because it is the eve of the triduum, the three most intense days of Lent. Our attention focuses even more closely on Jesus. We hang on his every word and action. This spiritual sums up best, what I believe our attitude should be at this time: "Hush, hush / Somebody's callin' my name / Oh, my Lord / What shall I do?" This is a time to deepen the silence before God.

We call to mind the first Wednesday in Lent on this the last Wednesday. We remember that we are dust. We call to mind that Jesus has been calling us to be and do a new thing. We will hear Jesus a lot better if we meditate and are still before him.

The Lenten journey has taken us across a whole religious landscape and worldview. The lessons we have paid attention to are life lessons. Bishop Barbara Harris said to me once during Lent, "If you have a bad habit to give up during Lent, you should give it up for the rest of your life."

It is quite likely that the callin' voice the slaves were referring to was someone calling them to escape from slavery. Makes perfect sense to equate such a voice with that of Jesus. Jesus calls us to freedom and to new life.

I suspect that this call often came at night. Yes, God calls us at night, oftentimes out of the darkness. "Hush, hush" reminds us that we need to be attentive. We have to pay close attention to hear the voice of God and what the tone says to us. Life hangs on the voice. Life hangs on the call to freedom. Life hangs on our readiness to follow the voice.

The theme of death is also present in this spiritual, and we have spent a lot of time reflecting on death. The singers of this song seem quite open to the presence and the coming of death. Death brings salvation. Once again, for the slaves death was probably a welcomed release from the misery of life. For them, death was their salvation.

As we journey into the last three days of Lent may we hear the voice of God, know the life of God through Jesus, find life through our suffering, and bring joy and peace to others. "Hush, hush!"

Spiritual Exercise

Read John 12:23-28, 35-36.

Take three ten-minute sessions today and be very still. Just desire to be in the presence of Jesus. Tell Jesus that you will walk with him over the next three days and thank him for all the good things he has done for you.

Before going to sleep tonight, spend some time reading over the passage from the Gospel of John.

- What is the silence whispering to you? What grows in the dark of your life?

- As you prepare for the last three days of Lent, to what do you look forward to most?

- Remember that there are new Christians around the world who will commit to Jesus during the next few days. Pray for them.

DAY **38** | MAUNDY THURSDAY

Let Us Break Bread Together

Let us break bread together on our knees;
Let us break bread together on our knees.
When I fall on my knees with my face to the rising sun,
Oh Lord, have mercy on me.

Let us drink wine together on our knees;
Let us drink wine together on our knees.
When I fall on my knees with my face to the rising sun,
Oh Lord, have mercy on me.

Traditional

When Jesus prayed to his Father in the Garden of Gethsemane, he did so on his knees. His heart breaking, he looked up to heaven and asked for God's mercy. We remember his humility, his fear, and his obedience. Perhaps mostly we remember his trust in God and God's plan for him.

When Jesus wanted to show the disciples what it means to know God and what it means to be God for each other, he did so on his knees. Taking their dusty feet into his open hands, he washed them. We remember their embarrassment, their discomfort, and their reluctance to be served. Perhaps, mostly, we remember Jesus' clarity and patience with them. "If I your Lord and master wash your feet. . . ."

Jesus' actions were shocking, because it was not his place as their teacher to do such an action. Jesus showed them that he was not tied to a place of privilege and gave them the best interpretation of the incarnation. God stoops to wash our feet.

We may feel that our money, our jobs, and our connections make us so important that we would never be caught kneeling to wash the feet of those in need. In our self-importance, we are sometimes too proud to kneel before the questions, challenges, and the servants in our lives. We sometimes forget that behind the dirty feet lies a grace-filled person searching our actions for a glimpse of Jesus. We need to ask for mercy, for the times we have failed to respond in humility.

On this day, "with our face to the rising sun," we kneel with the community of servants. As we kneel before the Lord's table and before one another, we recognize the importance of God's mercy. We are servants because Jesus commanded us to go and wash the feet of others. To wash the feet of others is to know where people have been, to know what they have gone through, and to put ourselves in their shoes.

The bread and wine offered today by Jesus reminds us of our unity in him. It is bread that is broken and wine that is shared. The sacrament of the presence of Jesus calls us to humility and an openness to be broken and shared.

To break bread together and to drink wine together is to remember Jesus' love for us and his commandment of love. Together, we remember Jesus on his knees and kneel down beside him. Together.

Spiritual Exercise

Read John 13:1-17. Try to imagine how difficult it would be to wash the feet of your boss, your next-door neighbor, a certain member of your family, or the homeless person in the center of the town.

You may ask a member of your family to have you wash his or her feet. When you are finished washing them, rub some lotion or oil on them.

Meditate on where your feet have taken you and ask God to bless your future journeys.

Repeat the spiritual slowly and lovingly.

Make an effort to get up early on Good Friday morning for prayer.

■ What does it mean to you to be the body of Christ in this world? What does it mean to be the blood of Jesus in this world?

■ How can your life take on the image of the kneeling servant Jesus?

■ Remember that Jesus was breaking with cultural and religious norms in washing his disciples feet.

■ Remember that Jesus is really present for you in the bread and the wine you receive in the Holy Supper.

DAY **39** | GOOD FRIDAY

Were You There?

Were you there when they crucified my Lord?
Were you there when they crucified my Lord?
Sometimes it cause me to tremble, tremble, tremble.
Were you there when they crucified my Lord?

Were you there when they nailed Him to the tree?
Were you there when they nailed Him to the tree?
Sometimes it causes me to tremble, tremble, tremble.
Were you there when they nailed Him to the tree?

Were you there when they laid Him in the tomb?
Were you there when they laid Him in the tomb?
Sometimes it causes me to tremble, tremble, tremble.
Were you there when they laid Him in the tomb?

Traditional

Good Friday was a great blow for the disciples of Jesus. They believed he was the Messiah, but they watched from a distance as he was crucified. Watching Jesus die like the worst of criminals must have shaken their faith in him and their faith in God. Surely, God would break the clouds and come down and save him. But nothing happened. Jesus died.

Only the eyes of faith can help us understand what happened on Good Friday. The early church struggled to make sense of the cross. They wanted to know what Jesus' death meant for them and for the whole world.

Good Friday still troubles us and leaves us with questions. "Were you there?" rings out the question of this spiritual. Oh, what an awful experience. "It causes me to tremble." Almost two thousand years after Jesus' death, the slaves could still tremble at what happened. What impact does the death of Jesus have on us?

The apostle Paul says it this way in Romans 6:3, 6: "Do you not know that all of us who have been baptized into Christ Jesus were baptized into his death? . . . We know that our old self was crucified with him, . . . and we might no longer be enslaved to sin." In the crucified Christ we can see the crucifixion of our sins. Every prejudice we cling to, every injustice we perpetrate, every excuse we offer, every pain we inflict is nailed there with Jesus. To take those nailed sins down off the cross is like submitting once again to a kind of slavery. If Jesus died to free us, why would we want to go back to the company of sins that enslave us?

God does not will human suffering. Enslaved by their anger, rage, and self-righteousness, the people crucified Christ. Enslaved by greed, power, and self-deception, people of America condoned enslavement of black people.

We cannot look at the events of Good Friday without asking pardon for our ongoing oppression of others. Like Jesus, we need to pray for the forgiveness of those who persecute us. And we need to ask God to forgive us of our sins and enlighten our minds so that we may know what we do.

"Were you there when they crucified my Lord?" echoes throughout our lives today. Where are we when others are oppressed? Where are we when others are victimized because of race, color, class, or sexual orientation?

We have been on a journey that has led us to the cross. Who sets out on a journey that leads to death? All of us. Our journey of life leads us to death and fortunately for us, we find Jesus there.

Spiritual Exercise

Read John 18:1—19:42; or read Mark 14:1—15:47. Spend some time in the courtyard with Jesus, visiting with him before his death. Say to him, "Jesus, I want to be there at the cross. Make me the beloved disciple who stands next to your mother."

In the Roman Catholic tradition, there is usually a meditation on the Five Sorrowful Mysteries: 1) The Agony in the Garden; 2) The Scourging at the Pillar; 3) The Crowning with Thorns; 4) The Carrying of the Cross; 5) The Crucifixion. Be present with Jesus at each of these mysteries and hear yourself tell Jesus that you love him.

- Where is the scandal of the cross in today's world? Where are you when people are being crucified?
- What does it mean for you to carry the cross? Why does Jesus choose not to save himself?
- Remember that we were there and that we are here.
- Remember that Jesus spent his last hours hanging between thieves and talking to them.

DAY **40** | HOLY SATURDAY/EASTER VIGIL

He 'Rose

They crucified my Savior and nailed Him to the tree,
They crucified my Savior and nailed Him to the tree,
They crucified my Savior and nailed Him to the tree,
And the Lord will bear my spirit home.
He 'rose, He 'rose, He 'rose from the dead!
He 'rose, He 'rose, He 'rose from the dead!
And the Lord will bear my spirit home.

Then Joseph begged His body and laid it in the tomb,
Then Joseph begged His body and laid it in the tomb,
Then Joseph begged His body and laid it in the tomb,
And the Lord will bear my spirit home.
He 'rose, He 'rose, He 'rose from the dead!
He 'rose, He 'rose, He 'rose from the dead!
And the Lord will bear my spirit home.

Sister Mary, she came running, a looking for the Lord,
Sister Mary, she came running, a looking for the Lord,
Sister Mary, she came running, a looking for the Lord,
And the Lord will bear my spirit home.
He 'rose, He 'rose, He 'rose from the dead!
He 'rose, He 'rose, He 'rose from the dead!
And the Lord will bear my spirit home.

An angel came from heaven and rolled the stone away,
An angel came from heaven and rolled the stone away,
An angel came from heaven and rolled the stone away,
And the Lord will bear my spirit home.
He 'rose, He 'rose, He 'rose from the dead!
He 'rose, He 'rose, He 'rose from the dead!

Traditional

The Easter Vigil Eucharist is one of the most splendid celebrations. We stand on the edge of Easter and get ready to say good-bye to Lent for now. During the liturgy, we recall the experience of the people of Israel and how the Lord saved them. Their salvation story is our salvation story.

Like the beginning of Lent, there is silence. In this liturgy more than any other, our silence meets the word of God. Even the celebrant is silent, since there is usually no homily. Silence borders on wonder on this night. Silence accompanies the waiting. Silence reminds us of our journey during these forty days. We stand in silence before our pain and before the glory of God.

We have journeyed with the slaves as they sang of life, freedom, and their hopes. They passed through their own desert and experienced many crucifixions. In the midst of suffering and pain they believed in God, goodness, and freedom. Believing that freedom would come, they held onto their faith in God. Their experience of suffering and salvation forms part of our story. In their liberty, we are all made free.

Often on this night, candidates are ready to be baptized and received in the Church. Families and friends gather to participate in the festival of word, light, and blessings. We listen to the biblical stories of our ancestors in faith.

The sting of Good Friday prevents the disciples from thinking back to all the hope and life that Jesus proclaimed. When Mary and the disciples look into the tomb, they are shocked. After all this, the tomb is empty? Is Jesus risen, or is this a trick?

Time will tell. Resurrections take time. But they happen. Sometimes we are called to remember redemption, remember the healing, and remember the love and the touch before we can experience the resurrection.

We remember all they endured and we think of our hardships as a nation, a people, and individuals: "Stony the road we trod / Bitter the chast'ning rod / Felt in the days when hope unborn had died / Yet with a steady beat / Have not our weary feet / Come to the place for which our fathers sighed?"

If we are fortunate, we are at a different place from where we started. We might even be shouting, "Free at last!" And if we are not quite there yet, we are still called to rejoice, still called to believe we will get there.

Now we get to proclaim "Alleluia!" Now we get to praise God and live out all that freedom brings. We get to sing the spirituals and live the spirituals, because they offer us great hope. Amen!

The Mourners, by Fred Flemister